Favorite OLD MASTER PAINTINGS from the

LOUVRE MUSEUM
Paris

Favorite OLD MASTER PAINTINGS from the

LOUVRE MUSEUM
Paris

INTRODUCTION AND COMMENTARIES BY

MICHEL LACLOTTE

Chief Curator Department of Painting
Louvre Museum, Paris

ADDITIONAL COMMENTARIES BY

JEAN-PIERRE CUZIN

Curator Department of Painting
Louvre Museum, Paris

ABBEVILLE PRESS, INC., PUBLISHERS • NEW YORK, N. Y.

On the JACKET:
Portrait of Mona Lisa by Leonardo da Vinci

TITLE PAGE
Moneychanger and His Wife by Quentin Massys

All photographs furnished by the
Service de documentation photographique de la
Réunion des musées nationaux, Paris, France

Library of Congress Catalog Number: 79–64988

ISBN 0-89659-065-8

CONTENTS

INTRODUCTION

"IT SEEMS TO ME that there is everything in the Louvre, that through it one can love and understand everything." Or again: "The Louvre is the book in which we learn to read." These statements by Cézanne—which could have been made by so many other artists—shed light on one of the essential missions of museums too often forgotten today in favor of more commonplace educational and particularly touristic functions: offering a constant reference for living art. Is not painting often, at least at the beginning of any career, meditation on painting? When periodically this or that artist raises the cry *"Burn the Louvre!"* it is less a rejection of a major symbol of tradition than an urgent response to a necessary parricide.

These roles of nourishing and of stimulating—even in the rejection they provoke—have been fulfilled by the Louvre since its opening in 1793 because of the multiplicity of examples it can offer the visual appetites of its visitors. Among the major museums of the world there are certainly others that own more complete series of this or that school, more significant masterpieces by this or that artist, but there are few that provide quite as varied a representation of European painting from Cimabue to the nineteenth century. Such diversity derives both from the history of the museum and from the manner in which its collections were established, and it distinguishes the Louvre from among the other great museums.

One might say, by oversimplifying, that museums can be divided into two categories. To the first belong those museums that have inherited the essential wealth of their holdings from a prince or ruling family. Such is the case of the Dresden and Vienna museums and those of Florence, as well as the Hermitage and the Prado. Museums of the second type, such as the former Kaiser-Friedrich Museum in Berlin, the National Gallery in London, or the Metropolitan Museum in New York—all founded in the nineteenth century—or the National Gallery in Washington—founded in the twentieth century—assembled their collections bit by bit through private donations and a regular acquisitions policy. The Louvre is the only one among

its peers to correspond simultaneously to both definitions. It owes its origin to a royal collection, that of the kings of France, which brought it some of those illustrious and irreplaceable works that are sometimes lacking in museums of the second type. But it has also been able to acquire thousands of paintings during the last two centuries and enrich its holdings more than those museums of royal origin that lack considerable financial means and access to private generosity. These endowments have not only increased the size of the Louvre's holdings; they have also slowly completed the prestigious but too partial (in both senses of the word) image that the collections formed before the nineteenth century gave of the painting of the past. Thus, one after another, have come the "primitives" of the various schools, and many of the numerous masters (among whom Vermeer, El Greco, and Georges de La Tour are the spectacular examples) forgotten during the classical centuries. Meanwhile, in successive waves from the Musée de Luxembourg (the museum of modern art of the period) and from large bequests, the painters of the nineteenth century came to join their great predecessors and models in the Louvre. Before being copied by Dufy, had not Renoir gone there to copy Delacroix, who himself had copied Titian and Rubens?

Let us sketch in broad strokes the principal stages in the long history by which the Louvre became what it is today.

Very little evidence remains of the pictures commissioned or acquired by the kings of France before the sixteenth century. It is to Francis I that credit must go for having truly founded the royal collections of paintings, collections assembled to satisfy the personal tastes of an enlightened sovereign and to illustrate the glory of his reign. As early as 1516, one year after his accession to the throne, the king invited to France the most famous artist of the time, Leonardo da Vinci. By the time of the artist's death in 1519, the royal collections featured several of his works, which constituted a unique group—one of the most precious treasures of the Louvre—around which slowly were gathered other masterpieces by the great artists of the Italian

Renaissance: Andrea del Sarto, Raphael, Titian, Sebastiano del Piombo. Henceforth the royal *cabinet de tableaux*, installed in the palace of Fontainebleau and only transferred to the palace of the Louvre in the seventeenth century, was maintained, admired, and visited as though it were already a museum. The rulers of the late sixteenth and early seventeenth centuries did little to enrich it. But at least Henri IV, and especially Marie de Médicis and Louis XIII, turned for the decoration of their residences to renowned European artists: Pourbus, Gentileschi and Rubens, Vouet and Poussin. Some important paintings that belonged to one or another of these decorative ensembles are in the Louvre today. They are dominated by the sumptuous canvases celebrating the merits of Marie de Médicis executed by Rubens between 1623 and 1625 for the Luxembourg palace.

Louis XIV, advised by his minister Colbert, decided when he assumed power in 1661 to enrich the *cabinet de tableaux* and make it a symbol, as Versailles would be, of the royal pomp that was to dazzle Europe. It is fair to say that this political motivation on the part of the king was complemented by a true collector's vocation. After purchasing a portion of the famous collection of Cardinal Mazarin and then the less remarkable one of the banker Jabach (containing certain Italian masterpieces from the collection of Charles I of England), he never ceased buying, commissioning, or receiving bequests of paintings that were to decorate the apartments of Versailles and the other royal palaces: works by his painters (Le Brun, Mignard, etc.), by great French artists of previous generations (Poussin, Claude, Valentin), and Italian paintings, often Bolognese, of the Seicento. Toward the end of the century, Dutch (Rembrandt) and Flemish (van Dyck, Rubens) paintings began to enter the royal collections, at a time when critics, collectors, and young painters were coming more and more to admire the great Flemish art of the beginning of the century and Rubens in particular. These moderns, "Rubenists" and champions of color, aligned themselves against the "Poussinists," who defended drawing.

When toward the end of Louis XIV's long reign an inventory of the *cabinet de tableaux* was taken (1709–10), it was found to contain, not counting copies and sketches, 1,478 paintings by masters (930 French, 369 Italian, 179 from the Northern schools)—a sumptuous collection, one of the richest in Europe at that time. Despite the presence of masterpieces by Rubens, van Dyck, Rembrandt, and Holbein, it was dominated by classical French painting and by the Italian painting that runs from Leonardo da Vinci and Titian to the School of Bologna.

Under Louis XV, purchases of pictures by masters were much less frequent. While some princes, such as the Duc d'Orléans, or financiers, like Crozat, set up admirable collections (from which the king of Prussia, the elector of Saxony, Catherine the Great, and English collectors would later be able to profit), and while auctions and the art market were developing in Paris, the king and his advisers neglected numerous opportunities for acquisition. The record of purchases and orders from living artists was fortunately more positive. Important canvases by, for example, Boucher, Lancret, Joseph Vernet, Chardin, de Nattier, and by certain portrait painters entered the royal collections—but nothing by Watteau.

Under the following reign, that of Louis XVI, there was a remarkable redressing of cultural policy. Commissions to living artists encouraged the rebirth of great "history painting" and thus the ripening of neoclassicism; and they enriched the royal collections, which henceforth were no longer restricted to the sole pleasure of the court but considered a national patrimony intended for the public. As early as 1750, mounting opinion had led to the showing in the Luxembourg palace of a selection of paintings drawn from the royal collections, and Diderot had suggested in the *Encyclopédie* (1765) the setting up of a true museum for the royal collections in the palace of the Louvre, where the court had not lived for almost a hundred years. The idea did not finally take shape until the Revolution. But in the meantime, Louis XVI's *directeur des bâtiments,* Comte d'Angiville, had considerably enlarged the collection of older paintings in a spirit of encyclopedic eclecticism, in order to fill gaps, repair omissions, and present a broader view of European painting. He thus completed the French series (Le Nain, Le Sueur), established a solid collection of paintings from the Northern schools (Rubens, Van Dyck, Jordaens, Rembrandt, Ruisdael, Terborch, etc.) and Spain (Murillo).

Under the revolutionary government, the Musée Central des Arts opened on August 10, 1793, in the Grande Galerie of the Louvre. The collections of the Académie Royale de Peinture et de Sculpture came to be added to the basic royal holdings. These collections contained, along with the "reception pieces" of the academicians, such as Watteau's *Pilgrimage to the Island of Cythera,* paintings seized from the homes of émigré collectors or confiscated as church property. In this way the *Virgin of Autun* by Jan van Eyck, some Flemish and Dutch cabinet pictures, the paintings from the studio of Isabella d'Este coming from Richelieu's château, some important religious canvases of the French seventeenth century, and Guardi's *Feasts* entered the Louvre.

Soon after began a period of adventure that for about fifteen years made the Louvre the most extraordinary museum of all time, through the influx of works of art taken in the wake of French victories in Belgium, Holland, Germany, and Italy. International morality today condemns such action. We would be wrong, however, to attribute it solely to the spirit of plunder characteristic of all victorious armies. Indeed, the organizers of the Musée Napoléon were surely dreaming of an ideal temple of the arts, which would be open to all the citizens of imperial Europe and symbolize the moral and intellectual achievements of the Revolution. This idealistic enterprise in support of the educational role of the work of art was extended to the provinces by the creation of other museums, supplied from Parisian sources, in the large provincial cities. At the Louvre itself, Vivant-Denon, the remarkable director of the Musée Napoléon, in his constant concern for encyclopedic knowledge, had sought to provide the most complete representation possible of the history of painting, by taking advantage of the spoils of conquest and by making numerous purchases. He was able to understand the importance of the "primitives," especially the Italian ones, hitherto quite neglected or even despised, and which only certain pioneers of taste were beginning to revive.

In 1815, after Waterloo, commissioners sent to Paris by all countries involved took back from the Louvre more than five thousand works of art. Only about a hundred paintings escaped repatriation, among them some Trecento and Quattrocento altarpieces deliberately left behind by the Florentine commissioners, and Veronese's *Marriage at Cana,* exchanged for a large canvas by Le Brun.

After a less active period, which nevertheless saw the creation of the Luxembourg museum (a collection devoted to works by living artists and later transferred to the Louvre) the Louvre began to grow again, following the Revolution of 1848 and under the Second Empire. The Louvre's exhibition space was considerably enlarged by the construction of new galleries, and the collections were expanded through a fortunate series of purchases covering all schools. Two major collections entered the Louvre at this time: that of the Marchese Campana, bought in its entirety in Rome in 1862, which, by including some one hundred Italian panels from the Trecento and Quattrocento, came at the right moment to fill out insufficient holdings in this area; and the collection of Dr. La Caze, bequeathed in 1869. Thanks to the La Caze donation, probably the most important in its history, the Louvre could finally display the French masters of the eighteenth century—after the eclipse of taste that had caused them to be forgotten—and strengthen its Flemish and Dutch holdings with additional masterpieces.

The period from the beginning of the Third Republic until the First World War was marked by a still more active policy of purchasing all kinds of old masters, from El Greco and Rogier van der Weyden to the *Pietà of Avignon*. By this time, art history had become a demanding discipline, and curators were diligent about classifying works, taking inventory, and assigning artists and movements to their proper place. During this period the Louvre acquired many important works by French painters of the nineteenth century, thanks to the periodic transfer of paintings from the Luxembourg, shrewd purchases, and above all, donations of entire collections, such as those of Thomas Thiéry (1902), Moreau-Nélaton (1906), and Chauchard (1909). Corot, Millet, the Barbizon painters, and Courbet thus joined the ranks of Géricault, Ingres, and Delacroix. At the same time, because of the generous bequests of Caillebotte (1894), Camondo (1911), and again, Moreau-Nélaton, Impressionist painting, so long rejected by official taste but recognized by enlightened collectors, began to enter the national collections.

After 1918, the financial resources of French museums noticeably diminished. The Louvre still managed to buy such pictures as Dürer's *Self-Portrait,* Courbet's *Studio*, and Delacroix's *Sardanapalus*. But despite effective help from the Société des Amis du Louvre, it failed to secure the countless masterpieces from French private collections that foreign museums and collectors, particularly American, were now able to acquire. On the eve of the Second World War, however, a new spirit breathed once more through the Louvre, which finally undertook a vast campaign of reorganization and acquired paintings by Georges de La Tour and the other seventeenth-century "painters of reality"—scarcely emerged from oblivion—as well as some relatively unknown works of the School of Fontainebleau. After the war, and while the necessary modernization of the museum was resumed, several large donations (the most striking of which was probably that of Carlos de Beistegui; while the most numerous and brilliant enlarged the museum's Impressionist holdings) proved the constancy, henceforth exceptional in Europe, of private French and foreign generosity toward the Louvre. Increased purchasing credits— and recently, new legal measures permitting the payment of inheritance taxes by donating works of art—have, on the other hand, encouraged the pursuit of a sustained acquisitions policy. It has thus been possible to expand several sections of French painting, from the primitives to the nineteenth century; to stress some aspects not yet represented of the work of certain artists (Georges de La Tour, Le Nain, Watteau, Fragonard); to introduce foreign masters (Sassetta, Wolf Huber, Terbrugghen, Piero della Francesca); to extend the English and Spanish holdings; and to begin to represent nineteenth-century schools of foreign painting seldom seen outside their native countries (Friedrich). All this, of course, has been done unsystematically, without an excess of pedantry—that is to say, by searching, above all, for the rare and beautiful work that will bring to the visitor what Poussin asks of painting: the "delight" of the eye and the mind.

MICHEL LACLOTTE

Favorite OLD MASTER PAINTINGS from the

LOUVRE MUSEUM
Paris

Cimabue (CENNI DI PEPI), c. 1240–1302, *Italian*

MADONNA AND CHILD ENTHRONED WITH ANGELS

DURING THE SECOND HALF of the thirteenth century, the pictorial language that was to become that of Europe for several centuries began to emerge in Tuscany. Before Giotto, who at the end of the century established a definitive new figurative conception, the great master was Cimabue, a Florentine who also worked in Rome, Pisa, and Assisi—the last an experimental center for the new painting. The chief source for his style and iconography was Byzantine art. But he profoundly transformed his models. As a contributor to the powerful Gothic current that was rediscovering the heritage of classical antiquity and of which the sculptor Nicola Pisano was the inspired champion, he cast off the rigid yoke of Byzantine academicism.

The Louvre *Madonna* is perhaps the most important thirteenth-century Italian painting existing outside Italy. It comes from the church of San Francesco in Pisa. Many recent scholars believe it to have been painted around 1270, before Cimabue's trip to Rome (1272), and not thirty years later, at the end of his life, as was once thought. The work thus precedes two other famous monumental altarpieces on the same theme, that of the Virgin and Child "enthroned in majesty" and surrounded by angels, both now in the Uffizi in Florence: the *Santa Trinità Maestà* also by Cimabue and the *Rucellai Madonna* (1285) by the Sienese Duccio. While adhering to a traditional compositional scheme that emphasizes the hieratic quality and solemn majesty of the divine group, Cimabue displays here a profoundly original plastic sensibility. He replaces Byzantine fixity with an entirely new suppleness, especially in the folds of the drapery. His subtlety of execution, radically different from the dry, opaque manner practiced by his Byzantinizing Italian predecessors, allows him to create nuances in the modeling and thus to suggest the reality of volumes in a luminous space. He thus paved the way for Duccio.

Panel 167 × 108⅝" (424 × 276 cm)

Giotto di Bondone, 1266/67–1337, *Italian*

SAINT FRANCIS ALTARPIECE

GIOTTO, HAILED BY DANTE for having renewed the art of painting, brought about a complete revolution in the representation of forms. He shattered the Byzantine tradition by constructing simple and massive volumes, clearly defined in space, while showing a concern for the faithful rendering of reality that astonished his contemporaries.

This Louvre panel, which, like Cimabue's *Madonna*, comes from the church of San Francesco in Pisa, is signed on the old frame. The principal composition shows Saint Francis miraculously receiving from Christ, who appears to him, the stigmata—the wounds on the hands, feet, and side that were inflicted on the Savior on the Cross. The three predella scenes represent other episodes from the saint's life: *The Dream of Innocent II* shows the sleeping pope dreaming that Francis is upholding the crumbling Church; *The Assignment of the Rule* depicts Francis and his companions receiving the rules of the Franciscan order from the pope; *Saint Francis Preaching to the Birds* illustrates one aspect of the saint's piety: his familiarity with and closeness to all divine creation.

The worship of Saint Francis, flourishing from the moment of the "poverello's" death in 1206, is illustrated particularly in the building of the two-level basilica in Assisi. The scenes from the *Life of Saint Francis*, painted in fresco in the upper basilica and traditionally held to be the work of Giotto, are today sometimes considered the painter's first great work, sometimes thought to be of doubtful attribution. But the composition of the four scenes of the Louvre altarpiece repeats, with variations, that of four of the Assisi frescoes. This constitutes a very strong argument in favor of the hypothesis that the frescoes are indeed by Giotto: it is hard to imagine the painter signing his name on the Louvre picture to the conceptions of another artist.

It is generally thought that, for the principal scene, Giotto left part of the execution to his assistant. The three predella episodes, however, which show delicate and subtle variations with respect to the Assisi frescoes, must be entirely by his hand.

Panel 123 ⅝ × 63 ¾" (314 × 162 cm)

Antonio Pisanello, c. 1394–1450/55, *Italian*
PORTRAIT OF GINEVRA D'ESTE

THE IDENTITY OF THIS FRAIL young princess has been much debated. The vase embroidered on the sleeve at the right is quite similar to the two-handled vase that constitutes the emblem of the house of Este, and which appears, for example, on the medal of Lionello d'Este, designed by Pisanello himself. Some have taken it to be a portrait of Margherita Gonzaga, wife of Lionello, or of her sister, Cecilia Gonzaga. The little sprig of juniper (*ginepro*) stitched on the shoulder suggests an even more tempting identification with Ginevra d'Este, who was born in 1419. At a very early age she married the terrible condottiere Sigismondo Malatesta, whose portrait in profile by Piero della Francesca is owned by the Louvre. The unfortunate girl was poisoned by her husband in 1440. The naïve and modest charm of the Louvre princess corresponds to the way one imagines her, knowing her tragic fate.

The profile view acts as a reminder that between 1438 and 1449 Antonio Pisanello worked at creating admirable likenesses on medals. Here the capricious and supple undulation of the lines, and the caressing sweetness of the modeling, show that Pisanello, a North Italian artist, remained under the spell of the International Gothic style, without being touched by the revolutionary teachings of the Florentines. The extravagance of the costume, with the high, depilated forehead—in accordance with the fashion of the time—and the background of dark foliage, with its scattered flowers and butterflies placed with scrupulous precision, seem to add to the young girl's reveries, while her fragile, almost Oriental charm helps to create an atmosphere of rare poetry.

The painting may date from around 1433, the period of Ginevra's betrothal to Malatesta, or a little later, around 1436–38.

Panel 16⅞ × 11¾″ (43 × 30 cm)

Fra Angelico (GUIDO DI PIETRO), c. 1400–1455, *Italian*

CORONATION OF THE VIRGIN

FRA ANGELICO'S PURELY religious inspiration, his quiet mysticism, and the delicacy of his colors have done as much as his monastic existence to create a persistent misunderstanding of his art, one upheld by the excessive uses to which it was put by the mawkishly devout imagery of the nineteenth century. Far from being isolated in the pious silence of his monastery, the artist was an active participant in the most daring formal experiments of his time. One of the foremost painters in Florence, he understood and absorbed the importance of the artistic revolution whose leaders were the architect Filippo Brunelleschi and the painter Masaccio. The *Coronation of the Virgin,* probably painted shortly before 1435, is the proof of this. The structure of the composition—the position and scale of the figures, the design of the pavement, and the foreshortening of the staircase—is established in accordance with an extremely skillful geometric double perspective, presupposing a perfect knowledge of the new architectonic conceptions of these pioneers. To convey his fervor, Fra Angelico thus uses the new language of the Renaissance, which allows a rational reconstruction of the visible world in a three-dimensional space. Lyricism and lucidity—it is to the balance he maintains between the two requirements of sensibility and intelligence that the artist owes the unique harmony of his style.

The altarpiece was painted for the church of the Dominican convent of San Domenico in Fiesole, where Fra Angelico was later to become prior. The predella narrates episodes in the life of Saint Dominic, founder of the order.

Panel 83⅛ × 83⅛" (211 × 211 cm)

18

Paolo Uccello, c. 1397–1475, *Italian*

BATTLE OF SAN ROMANO

THIS MELEE OF HORSEMEN and foot soldiers illustrates an actual historical event: the battle between the Florentines and Sienese at San Romano in 1432, which ended in a Florentine victory. The episode represented here is the attack led by Micheletto da Cotignola, one of the Florentine captains. Two other panels of the same dimensions, in the National Gallery in London and the Uffizi Gallery in Florence, show other aspects of the same battle. The three paintings were originally joined to form a triptych and decorated a room in the Medici Palace (today the Palazzo Medici-Riccardi) in Florence. They are usually dated around 1455.

Older than most of the Renaissance pioneers, Uccello had rallied to their new ideas with all the enthusiasm of a convert. In composing the *Battle of San Romano,* he subjects a tangle of volumes to the strict laws of linear perspective, while playing in virtuoso fashion with stereometric devices for increased stylization and provocative foreshortening. The effect of such a play of pure forms must have been heightened by the glitter of the armor, painted with silver leaf (now tarnished). The rhythm of the lances gives coherence and monumental structure to this skillful composition, and above all the artist has imbued his *ballet mécanique* with a remarkable poetry, expressed in the disquieting looks that filter through the helmets. It should come as no surprise that Cubists and Surrealists have by turns been fascinated by these paintings.

Like a great number of other fourteenth- or fifteenth-century works in the Louvre, this picture comes from the Campana Collection. The Marchese Campana, an enthusiastic Roman collector, was the director of the state pawnbroker's office in Rome. Accused of embezzlement, he was imprisoned and his collection confiscated. It contained thousands of ancient objects and sculptures, as well as an important group of Italian primitives, assembled at a time when a taste for these artists was still rare. The entire Campana Collection was bought by the French government in 1862. The Louvre kept a portion of the Italian primitives, but starting in 1863 more than three hundred other pictures were distributed among ninety provincial museums. Recently this incomparable collection has been reassembled in a special museum in the Petit Palais in Avignon.

Panel 70⅞ × 124⅜" (180 × 316 cm)

Andrea Mantegna, 1430/1431–1506, *Italian*

CRUCIFIXION

TRAINED IN THE EXCITING atmosphere of Padua, with its fascination with antiquity, Mantegna based his work on the study of authentic ancient sculpture, seeking thereby to rediscover the historical truth of the sacred episodes he recounts. Such concern was unknown to previous artists, and it is illustrated in the *Crucifixion* by the accuracy of the Roman soldiers' gear. It is not a question of a sterile archaeological reconstitution, however, but of a powerful and impassioned recreation of the classical world. It is a grandiose vision that reinvents a universe of tragic statues and mineral landscapes through the simultaneously objective and distorting prism of perspective, here employed with astonishing audacity.

The Louvre *Crucifixion* is not an easel picture. It constituted the center of the predella of a large altarpiece, painted by Mantegna between 1457 and 1459 for the church of San Zeno in Verona, where the three principal panels, *Virgin and Child Surrounded by Saints,* are to be found. The other two panels of the predella, *Christ in the Garden of Olives* and the *Resurrection,* are in the Tours museum. The whole altarpiece was on display there under the Empire, but the commissioners in charge of repatriating works of art from the Veneto left only the predella in France.

The San Zeno Altarpiece, which exercised a considerable influence on many North Italian artists until the end of the fifteenth century, is the masterpiece of Mantegna's maturity, coming after his frescoes (nearly all destroyed) for the Ovetari Chapel in the Church of the Eremitani in Padua and just before he settled in Mantua.

Panel 26⅜ × 36⅝" (67 × 93 cm)

Giovanni Bellini, c. 1430–1516, *Italian*

CHRIST BLESSING

THE SUBJECT TREATED HERE by Bellini, a half-length figure of Christ giving a blessing and showing his wounds after the Resurrection, is much less common than the comparable one of the dead Christ seen half-length in the tomb and supported by angels. The painting belongs to the period in Giovanni Bellini's career, around 1465–70, when his style showed, by the hard modeling of forms and a concern for harsh grandeur, the close influence of his brother-in-law Mantegna. One can even see here connections with Flemish art, particularly with the tense and powerful style of Van der Weyden. And yet the subtlety of expression in the face, suffering and anxious but radiating goodness, belongs only to Bellini's art. The soft light bathing the forms and the delicate colors of the landscape and twilight sky where thin clouds extend show that Bellini's prime concern is for atmospheric unity; he thus directly opens the way to Giorgione, Titian, and the great Venetian colorists. Bellini, a daring innovator, is perhaps of all the painters of the Quattrocento the one whose work had the richest consequences for the art of the next centuries.

The Louvre painting, acquired in 1912, may be the *Savior Blessing* described by the historian Ridolfi in 1648 as belonging to the Augustinian monks of Santo Stefano in Venice, and which Bellini himself was said to have given to their monastery.

Panel 22⅞ × 17⅜" (58 × 44 cm)

Antonello da Messina, c. 1430–1479, *Italian*

PORTRAIT OF A MAN ("Il Condottiere")

AMID ALL THE FERMENT that made the fifteenth century in Italy one of the richest and most inventive periods in the history of painting, one must not overlook the Flemish contribution. Some of the major painters of the Quattrocento, such as Piero della Francesca, Giovanni Bellini, and Antonello da Messina, understood what the Northern masters had to offer: a sharper and more objective attention to reality, along with the technical means (the use of oil as a medium) to give form to this more realistic mode of perception. Sicilian-born Antonello, trained in Naples, must surely have studied the Flemish masterpieces to be found in that city; all his paintings bear traces of this. But he also absorbed the geometric teachings of the Florentine Renaissance. The Louvre portrait by Antonello, a three-quarter pose behind a parapet like those of Jan van Eyck, gives an impression of intense physical presence, and the artist thereby comes to resemble his Flemish exemplar. At the same time, he imparts to the volumetric structure a rigor of synthesis and a monumentality that are purely Italian.

The proudly resolute expression enlivening this portrait, one of the most striking of the twelve that Antonello painted, has led to its being known as *Il Condottiere*. Actually it is the portrait of a Venetian nobleman. The work dates from the fruitful time (1475–76) the artist spent in Venice, where he painted portraits and religious pictures that exercised a decisive influence on the new Venetian painting.

The picture was acquired in 1865, at the sale of the Pourtalès Collection.

Panel 13¾ × 11" (35 × 28 cm)

Sandro Botticelli, c. 1445–1510, *Italian*

VENUS AND THE GRACES OFFERING GIFTS TO A YOUNG GIRL

THIS WORK OFFERS A precious example of fresco, a technique essential to Italian painting of the fourteenth and fifteenth centuries, but which by its nature is seldom represented in museums outside Italy. It has as its companion piece a composition showing a young man before the assembled Arts. The two frescoes were discovered in 1873 under whitewash in the Villa Lemmi near Florence. After being detached from the wall, they were bought by the Louvre in 1882.

Since there is doubt as to who the owners of the villa were in Botticelli's time, several hypotheses have been proposed concerning the identity of the central figures in each of the two frescoes—probably a young married couple. It is no longer certain that they are Lorenzo Tornabuoni and his young wife, Giovanna degli Albizzi, as was long believed.

Though the subject is more complex than the simple representation of a young girl receiving her bridal veil from Venus accompanied by the three Graces, there are no further clues to the exact meaning of the mythological allegory. Probably it reflects the ideas on love developed by the circle of Neoplatonic humanists grouped around Marsilio Ficino and under the patronage of Lorenzo the Magnificent. We know that Botticelli frequented this group. In any case, with its dancing rhythm, friezelike composition, and subtle elegance, the work comes close to the *Primavera* (1477), especially if we assume that the background, now almost effaced, showed the vegetation of a garden. Scholars generally assign these frescoes to the years 1480–83, either shortly before or shortly after the large frescoes painted by Botticelli in the Sistine Chapel in Rome (1481–82).

Fresco 83½ × 111¾" (212 × 284 cm)

Leonardo da Vinci, 1452–1519, *Italian*

PORTRAIT OF MONA LISA ("La Gioconda")

A LEGENDARY PICTURE, the portrait of the Gioconda has given rise to countless and often rapturous observations and hypotheses—above all, hypotheses about the model's identity. Is it really Mona Lisa, who was born in Florence in 1479 and in 1495 married Francesco del Giocondo, an important Florentine citizen? This has been disputed, but it would seem reasonable to accept it. If this is the case, then the portrait was painted by Leonardo around 1503–6, when he returned for some years to Florence after a long stay in Milan.

Critics agree that beyond capturing the likeness of a particular Florentine lady, Leonardo painted the ideal image of the perfect human being, whose smile expresses the "movements of the soul." The landscape behind her presents a synthesized view of the visible world, one which affirms the Renaissance dream of universalism, whose most conscious interpreter was Leonardo da Vinci.

When, after another stay in Milan, Leonardo went to France in 1517 at the invitation of Francis I, he took the *Gioconda* with him. Bought by the king directly from the artist, or from his heirs at his death in 1519, the painting was always considered to be one of the most precious jewels in the royal collections. Its fame was revived in the nineteenth century by all the literary exegeses, especially in the Symbolist period, and it increased again when the theft of the picture in 1911 caused an international sensation. Stolen by an Italian workman, the painting was recovered two years later, unharmed, in Florence.

Having become a universally recognized symbol, the *Gioconda* has provoked and continues to provoke a mass of visual reinterpretations, from the bracing irreverence of Marcel Duchamp and Salvador Dali, and the manipulations of Kineticism and Pop Art, to the ludicrous caricatures that have made her an inexhaustible star of advertising.

Panel 30¼ × 20⅞" (77 × 53 cm)

Leonardo da Vinci, 1452–1519, *Italian*

VIRGIN AND CHILD WITH SAINT ANNE

THE LOUVRE OWNS AS MANY paintings by Leonardo da Vinci as all other museums in the world combined—that is to say, five or six out of the ten or twelve that can be assigned to him with relative certainty. It is in part to Francis I, who invited the painter to France—where he died in 1519—that we owe this unique grouping: the king probably owned the *Virgin of the Rocks*, the portrait of a young woman known as *La Belle Ferronnière*, and the *Saint John the Baptist*, and certainly the *Mona Lisa* and the *Virgin and Child with Saint Anne*. This last painting left the royal collection, most likely at the end of the sixteenth century, and was taken back to Italy. It was bought in 1629 in Casale Monferrato in the Piedmont by Cardinal Richelieu, and bequeathed by him in 1636 to Louis XIII.

Often called simply *Saint Anne*, the picture figures among the most important in Leonardo's career. The artist first executed the cartoon, different in composition, around 1498 in Milan; it is now in the National Gallery in London. A second cartoon, executed in Florence, has been lost. The Louvre picture was probably painted around 1510 in Milan; it remained unfinished, which explains the extremely light and transparent appearance of many parts of the painted surface.

The iconography of the theme chosen by Leonardo is somewhat unusual, but it occurs in the Middle Ages and survives in northern Europe until the seventeenth century. The artist may have been drawn to this representation, in which the Virgin is seated on her mother's knees, by its very strangeness: the bodies of the two women appear to form only a single body with multiple limbs. The Virgin seems to be trying to restrain the infant Jesus from straddling the lamb, symbol of sacrifice. A famous analysis by Sigmund Freud discerned in the blue cloak of the Virgin the outline of a vulture with outspread wings: Leonardo had recorded a fantasy in which a vulture had attacked him when he was a baby in his cradle.

This picture, often copied or imitated by Leonardo's followers, preserves intact its power of dream and emotion. This spellbinding and troubling image will always be disturbing because of its smiling faces marked by a strange sweetness, and because of its otherworldly landscape with steep cliffs bathed in tones of milky blue.

Panel 66⅞ × 50¾" (170 × 129 cm)

Raphael (RAFFAELLO SANZIO), 1483–1520, *Italian*
LA BELLE JARDINIÈRE

DURING HIS STAY IN FLORENCE (1504–8), Raphael painted ten or so Madonnas that rank among the most glorious of his works. Among the most outstanding, three are often compared: the *Madonna del Prato* or *Virgin of the Belvedere* (1506, Vienna, Kunsthistorisches Museum), the *Madonna del Cardellino* ("Virgin of the Goldfinch"; 1507, Florence, Uffizi), and *La Belle Jardinière* in the Louvre, also dated 1507. The three pictures show, in a vertical format, the Virgin seated in a landscape with the infant Jesus and the little Saint John the Baptist. They represent the moment when Raphael achieved a harmonious synthesis between the art—all sweetness and soft tranquillity—that he had inherited from his teacher Perugino, and the powerful, monumental style based on the clear organization of heavy and organically connected figures in space, which derived from the strong impression made on him by the works of Leonardo da Vinci. In *La Belle Jardinière*, the pyramidal composition, the supple arabesque linking the body of the child to the arms of his mother, and the design of the folds of the blue cloak are typical of this influence of Leonardo's work on the young Raphael.

The painter prepared the picture by several drawings and an overall cartoon, which today is in the collection of the Earl of Leicester at Holkham Hall in England. The work is signed in gold letters on the hem of the Virgin's cloak, above her foot, and dated near her elbow.

La Belle Jardinière, which owes its popular nickname, already current in the eighteenth century, to its pastoral landscape, may in the sixteenth century have been part of the collection of Francis I at the palace of Fontainebleau. The king certainly owned two of the most important Raphaels in the Louvre, the *Saint Michael* and the *Holy Family*, large pictures painted in 1518 and offered to him by Lorenzo de' Medici. The first definite mention of the picture as being in the royal collections appears in 1666. Ever since the opening of the Louvre, it has been one of the masterpieces most admired by French painters and connoisseurs. Ingres and his followers no doubt appreciated its musical purity of line and its firm and rounded modeling, but paradoxically it was Delacroix, the Romantic, who copied the figure of the infant Jesus and was inspired by the picture for his *Virgin of the Harvests* (1819, church of Orcemont, near Paris), one of his earliest canvases, which he painted when he was twenty-one.

Panel 48 × 31½" (122 × 80 cm)

Raphael (RAFFAELLO SANZIO), 1483–1520, *Italian*

PORTRAIT OF BALDASSARE CASTIGLIONE

CALLED "The best knight in the world" by the Emperor Charles V, Baldassare Castiglione (1478–1529) was the perfect type of Renaissance gentleman. A diplomat, humanist, and man of letters, he wrote *Il Cortigiano,* a celebrated work upholding the idea of a harmonious society ruled by reason and love, in the sense given to "love" in Neoplatonic circles. Raphael shares this ideal of aesthetic and spiritual perfection, and he illustrates it directly in the way he portrays Castiglione, transforming his likeness into the embodiment of a moral attitude. The profound affinity, both intellectual and emotional, linking the painter and his model explains this symbiosis.

A recent cleaning has revealed the picture's extraordinary delicacy of execution, with its subtle range of grays and refined lighting. It has often been observed that Raphael, as in some of his other portraits, has here kept in mind the pose of the *Mona Lisa*. The portrait was probably painted in Rome in 1514 or 1515, while Raphael was engaged in his great works for the Vatican.

Taken from Italy to Holland at the beginning of the seventeenth century, it was sold in Amsterdam, went from there to Madrid, and then to Paris, where it was bought for the collection of Cardinal Mazarin. It was acquired in 1661 from the cardinal's heirs, along with two other Raphaels, *Saint George* and *Saint Michael,* for the collection of Louis XIV. One indication of the admiration that the work has always aroused is that a number of artists have made copies of it—among others, Rembrandt (a drawing in the Albertina in Vienna), Rubens (London, Seilern Collection), and Matisse.

Canvas 32¼ × 26⅜" (82 × 67 cm)

Titian (TIZIANO VECELLIO), c. 1487–1576, *Italian*
CONCERT CHAMPÊTRE

THE *CONCERT CHAMPÊTRE* offers a famous example of true Venetian lyricism, that sensuousness achieved by the painters of sixteenth-century Venice, who juxtaposed the forms of female nudes and those of nature in a single warm and vibrant atmosphere. Painted around 1510, it is one of the very first examples of this grand style, which was to bring forth so many mythological or pastoral evocations and which continued to inspire painters all over Europe in the course of the following centuries. Manet's *Déjeuner sur l'herbe* may be one of its last transpositions.

The importance of the work explains why the hotly debated subject of its attribution deserves more attention than would a mere quarrel among scholars. Should we assign the picture to Giorgione, as has traditionally been done? Or should one see here a work by the young Titian? He was, of course, still under the influence of his teacher, who died prematurely in 1510. But he was already personal in his naturalistic spirit and the vitality with which he imbues this most mysteriously poetic of "musical interludes." Like most recent scholars, we prefer this second hypothesis, while also rejecting a third possibility, that the work was left unfinished by Giorgione and completed by Titian (though this would seem to be the case of the *Venus* in the Gemäldegalerie in Dresden).

The painting entered the royal collections in 1671. It had been in the collections of the Gonzaga family in Mantua, who owned many paintings by Titian. There are those who maintain that it originally belonged to Isabella d'Este, Marchesa of Gonzaga, but this claim has never been substantiated.

Canvas 43¼ × 54¾" (110 × 138 cm)

Titian (TIZIANO VECELLIO), c. 1487–1576, *Italian*

ENTOMBMENT OF CHRIST

THE GONZAGA COLLECTIONS in Mantua, from which the *Concert Champêtre* came, contained several other important canvases by Titian that in the seventeenth century passed into the collection of Charles I, and later into that of Louis XIV. The crowning glory of this magnificent group was undoubtedly the *Entombment*. As early as 1667, Philippe de Champaigne discoursed on its merits during one of the famous lecture-debates organized by Le Brun, where the doctrines of the Académie Royale de Peinture et de Sculpture were formulated and debated à propos of one or another of the pictures in the royal collections. Van Dyck, Rubens, Géricault, and Delacroix are among the many artists who studied the painting in Mantua, England, or Paris and made interpretations or copies of it as a spur to their own experiments.

The work, probably painted at the request of Marchese Federico Gonzaga, son of Isabella d'Este, is usually dated around 1523–25. After his initial "Giorgionesque" period, Titian had shown his capacity for monumental achievement in the *Assumption Altarpiece* for the Church of the Frari (1516–18), already Baroque in inspiration. With the *Entombment,* he returns to an entirely classical arrangement in the rhythm of harmoniously balanced forms placed in a frieze, and some scholars have seen in this a reflection of Raphael's *Deposition* (Rome, Galleria Borghese). But one should not try to push the similarity too far. Titian's vision is fundamentally dramatic; it rests on a lucid but impassioned play of expressive and formal contrasts, on a prodigious dialogue between light and shadow, dissolving in the tragic illumination of twilight. The *Entombment* is perhaps the first painting in his long career where Titian evokes pain and death; much later he will again take up the subject with more violently emotional accents.

Canvas 58¼ × 80¾" (148 × 205 cm)

Correggio (ANTONIO ALLEGRI), c. 1494–1543, *Italian*

SLEEPING VENUS

ALTHOUGH TRADITIONALLY designated as a ''Sleeping Antiope,'' the picture actually represents a *Sleeping Venus with Cupid Surprised by a Satyr.* It is under this title that it is mentioned in the Gonzaga collections in Mantua (from there, it followed the customary route: Charles I, Jabach, Mazarin, Louis XIV) together with another Correggio work, the *Education of Cupid* (now in the National Gallery in London). This common origin has led to the assumption that the two canvases were conceived as companion pieces and symbolized the two aspects of love: spiritual love (the *Education of Cupid)* and carnal love (the *Sleeping Venus*). The Louvre painting has also been compared to a series of famous mythological compositions (*Danaë,* Rome, Galleria Borghese; *Leda,* Berlin-Dahlem; *Jupiter and Io,* Vienna, Kunsthistorisches Museum) narrating the loves of Jupiter and which were given in part by Duke Federico Gonzaga to the Emperor Charles V. Be that as it may, all these canvases share the same sensual and refined character and date from the same period.

The *Sleeping Venus* is generally placed around 1525–26. This is the time of Correggio's full maturity, when, after the tour de force of the frescoes for the cupola of San Giovanni Evangelista in Parma, he goes on to display the unlimited resources of his virtuosity in those for the dome; such a whirling treatment of space will not be seen again until the most daring of Baroque ceilings. There is the same blending of forms in a luminous atmosphere and the same pictorial fluidity in the *Sleeping Venus*. It, like Correggio's other mythological idylls, echoes those of Giorgione and Titian (he was able to see them in the Gonzaga collections in Mantua), but with a wholly new accent. Isolated in Parma, Correggio invented a new *frisson* in painting, an evocation of voluptuousness that was to answer the dreams of the Romantics.

Canvas 74¾ × 48⅞" (190 × 124 cm)

Rosso Fiorentino (GIAN BATTISTA DI JACOPO), 1494–1540, *Italian*

PIETÀ

THE REFINED AND COMPLEX art of the Florentine Gian Battista di Jacopo, known as Rosso Fiorentino, one of the leading Italian Mannerists, was especially pleasing to the French king Francis I, to whom Rosso's work had been recommended by Aretino. He made the artist his court painter in 1532, granted him various privileges, and even bestowed on him the honorary title of "canon of the Sainte Chapelle." "Maître Roux" (Master Redhead), as the French called him, painted many fresco decorations for the palace of Fontainebleau, of which those in the gallery of Francis I still remain, and he was to die in France. The *Pietà* now in the Louvre is the only certain picture from Rosso's French period. It was painted for Duc Anne de Montmorency, constable of France, for the chapel of his castle in Écouen, north of Paris; we do not know exactly how it was situated in this chapel.

The dramatic power derived from Michelangelo here acquires a new and controlled strength in Rosso, whose art is usually more violent and contracted. The composition, with its shallow depth, suggests a bas-relief. The twisted elegance of a conception that stretches the human forms, carves the ringlets of hair, and fragments the folds of the garments, and the splendor of an unreal coloring that revels in purple, yellow, orange, and green tones, were too innovative to have much influence on French art. It would be necessary to wait for Delacroix, who, in his *Pietà* for the church of Saint-Denis-du-Saint-Sacrement in Paris, was to recall the gesture of grief of the Virgin's widespread arms.

Panel 49¼ × 62⅝" (125 × 159 cm)

44

Paolo Veronese, 1528–1588, *Italian*

THE MARRIAGE AT CANA

THE LOUVRE OWNS AN important series of paintings by Veronese, whose serene abundance and sumptuous balance doubtless correspond better to French taste, long dominated by classicism, than the anguish and anxiety of Tintoretto, who is consequently less well represented in the collections. Louis XIV owned several of Veronese's masterpieces, in particular *The Feast in the House of Simon,* a gift of the Republic of Venice, which adorns one of the salons in the palace of Versailles. The huge canvas of *The Marriage at Cana* was transported from Venice in 1799 for the Louvre; it remained in Paris in 1815, thanks to an agreement with the Austrian authorities, in exchange for *The Feast in the House of Simon* by Charles Le Brun.

The work, commissioned in 1562, was completed the following year in order to decorate the refectory of the Benedictine monastery on the island of San Giorgio in Venice. As in his other immense sacred banquets, such as *The Feast in the House of Levi* in the Accademia in Venice, Veronese uses the Gospel narrative in order to demonstrate his genius as a scene painter. He erects luminous architectural settings of porticoes, colonnades, and staircases, inspired by those of Palladio and placed in accordance with several points of perspective. They are peopled with lavish multitudes (here there are no less than 132 figures), overcrowded but harmoniously arranged. The religious scene, as represented here, has taken on the appearance of a fashionable feast. This impression is supported by the tradition that identified some of the wedding guests on the left as the great princes of the time (among others, Francis I, Charles V, and Suleiman the Magnificent), and among the musicians, Titian, Tintoretto, Bassano, Palladio, and Veronese himself.

Canvas 262⅛ × 389¾" (666 × 990 cm)

Jacopo Tintoretto, 1518–1594, *Italian*

PARADISE

THIS CANVAS CONSTITUTES the sketch for the *Paradise* painted by Tintoretto to decorate the back wall of the Grand Council chamber of the Doges' Palace in Venice, a gigantic composition often considered the largest existing painting on canvas. We know that after the fire of 1577, which destroyed much of the hall, a contest was organized on the subject of Paradise, the same as that of the damaged composition by Guariento that had to be replaced. Four sketches have come down to us: Veronese's (Lille museum), Jacopo Bassano's (Leningrad, Hermitage), Palma Giovane's (Milan, Ambrosiana), and the present picture. Veronese and Bassano won the competition, but they were unable to execute the work; upon Veronese's death in 1588, Tintoretto was commissioned to do it.

Despite the large number of figures, Tintoretto's skillful grasp of order prevents the work from becoming a disorganized swarm. On clouds around the central group representing the Coronation of the Virgin by Christ are arranged the twelve Apostles, the Fathers of the Church, the Patriarchs, and male and female saints—martyrs, soldier saints, bishops, founders of orders. To the left one can see the two nude figures of Adam and Eve. Whereas the large composition in Venice, dark in color, and somewhat confusing and heavy in its distribution of masses, is a little disappointing, the sketch in the Louvre shows clearly Tintoretto's first idea: large concentric curves revolving around the central group in a free and open rhythm of dark and lighted areas, executed in a dazzling, whirling style, with virulent, almost electric colors bursting with strident combinations of blue, bright pink, and yellow.

Canvas 56¼ × 142½" (143 × 362 cm)

Annibale Carracci, 1560–1609, *Italian*

FISHING

FRENCH PAINTERS, writers, and collectors have always shown a preference for Bolognese painting of the seventeenth century, and it constitutes one of the sources of their classicism. This explains the richness of the Bolognese collection in the Louvre, where all the great masters of this school—Carracci, Domenichino, Albani, Guercino—are represented by masterpieces. *Fishing* and its companion piece, *Hunting,* were given to Louis XIV in 1665 by Prince Camillo Pamphili.

Fishing and *Hunting* offer the most important evidence of Annibale Carracci's work as a landscape painter during the early part of his career, which he spent in Bologna with his cousin Lodovico. The bold experimentation of his work from this period—in sacred and profane subjects, genre scenes, landscapes, and portraits—brought forth a new pictorial language that spread from Rome and became fundamental to all painting of the seventeenth century.

The insipid and conventional uses to which many academic painters later put this style should not blind us to its true nature. It began as a form of naturalism seeking to free itself from the artifice and preciosity of Mannerism, for the same reasons (though not by the same means) as the style of Caravaggio and his followers. *Fishing,* probably painted around 1587–88, is a pure landscape, far removed from the fantastic visions of the Mannerists (such as those conceived by Nicolò dell'Abbate), and free as well of any literary allusions.

Canvas 53½ × 99⅝" (136 × 253 cm)

Michelangelo Caravaggio, c. 1573–1610, *Italian*

THE DEATH OF THE VIRGIN

OUR OWN DAY HAS NO monopoly on artistic scandals; the notion of an ''avant-garde'' holds true for all times. It was obviously not only by the disorder of his stormy life that Caravaggio shocked his contemporaries, but also by the revolutionary novelty of his art: its naturalism seemed literally intolerable to conservative circles while it enraptured and profoundly influenced the young painters who came from all over Italy to work in Rome, the art capital of the seventeenth century.

Commissioned, probably in 1605, for a chapel in the church of Santa Maria della Scala in Trastevere in Rome by the jurist Laerzio Cherubini, *The Death of the Virgin* was rejected by the clergy, who found Caravaggio's portrayal of the Virgin indecent, with her ''swollen appearance and her bare legs.'' It is, on the contrary, the dignity and tragic grandeur of the work that strike us today. We know that it also aroused the admiration of Roman artists, and at their request it was publicly exhibited for a week in April 1607, before being shipped to the Duke of Mantua. He had bought it from Cherubini at the urging of Rubens himself, then living in Rome and employed by the duke.

Caravaggio soon had to flee Rome. His wanderings led him from Naples to Malta, to Sicily, again to Naples, and finally ended miserably with his death in Porto Ercole on the eve of his rehabilitation and return to Rome.

Along with a great part of the Gonzaga collections, *The Death of the Virgin* was bought by Charles I of England twenty years after it was painted, and later passed with other works into the collection of the banker Jabach, then in 1671 into that of Louis XIV.

Canvas 145¼ × 96½" (369 × 245 cm)

Francesco Guardi, 1712–1792, *Italian*

THE DOGE RETURNING FROM THE LIDO ON THE *BUCINTORO*

THIS PICTURE IS part of a series of twelve canvases (eight in the Louvre, the other four in the museums of Grenoble, Nantes, and Brussels) illustrating successive episodes in the election of a doge in Venice. Traditionally the occasion called for a series of official feasts and popular celebrations that took place at the basilica of San Marco, at the Doges' Palace, in the Piazza San Marco, and at various other important places in the city. Lively observation, an accurate evocation of atmosphere—such are the visual qualities by which Guardi captures in these pictures the poetry of an eyewitness who knows that these are perhaps the last such celebrations in the twilight of a long history.

After the ceremony of marriage with the sea and a mass in the church of San Nicolò on the Lido, we see here the doge and his entourage reembarking on that astonishing ship, the *Bucintoro*—a veritable red and gold Rococo monument—beneath a canopy that extends from the church to the pier.

For these canvases, Guardi was inspired by compositions (drawings or paintings engraved by Brustolon) by Antonio Canaletto, the other great Venetian *vedutista,* or view-painter, of the eighteenth century. But his style is entirely personal; he has applied color in sparkling little touches with incomparable sureness and skill. The whole landscape, water and sky, is bathed in a diaphanous luminosity. The flickering quality of such a vision suggests in places—for the comparison is often overdone—the fleeting vibrations of the Impressionists.

This series of celebrations most likely represents the election of Doge Alviso IV Mocenigo in 1763, though Guardi may not have painted it until some ten years later.

Canvas 26⅜ × 39⅜" (67 × 100 cm)

Jan van Eyck, c. 1390–1441, *Italian*

MADONNA WITH CHANCELLOR ROLIN

FORESHADOWED BY THE advances made by Franco-Flemish miniaturists at the beginning of the fifteenth century (the Limbourg brothers, the Master of the Boucicaut Hours), who were already able to observe and transcribe acutely certain aspects of nature, a new perception of reality emerged in Flanders around 1420. It was due to the simultaneous appearance, at the very same time as Masaccio's appearance in Florence, of two exceptional artists: the Master of Flémalle (Robert Campin) and Jan van Eyck. But unlike the naturalism of the Florentines, which is of an intellectual order, that of the Flemish appeals to pure visual sensibility. Van Eyck sets down what his eye registers; the painting becomes the mirror of his life. But—and herein lies the Eyckian miracle—the trap of trompe-l'oeil is always avoided, thanks to the synthesis, the total vision, that the artist is able to impose. It is due also, of course, to the spiritual intensity with which he infuses his inventory of the world.

In the *Madonna with Chancellor Rolin,* the most insignificant detail of the landscape, barely perceptible, is painted with incredible exactness, and yet the whole of the composition is clear and harmonious. The technical perfection of the execution, which no other artist was to achieve, obviously allows such subtleties. Van Eyck's fidelity to reality does not, however, prevent him from constructing an imaginary architecture—or at least a noncontemporary one, since it belongs to the remote Roman repertory—nor from reconstituting a fictitious urban landscape, borrowed from various places (especially Liège) that he had visited.

The painting represents Nicolas Rolin, chancellor of Burgundy, an important figure at the court of Philip the Good, who reigned simultaneously over Flanders and the present Burgundy. It was probably executed for the chancellor in 1435. In 1800 it was transported from the collegiate church of Autun to the Louvre. Another Flemish masterpiece commissioned by Rolin has remained in place: the *Polyptych of the Last Judgment* (the *Beaune Altarpiece)* by Rogier van der Weyden, still in the Hôtel-Dieu in Beaune.

Panel 26 × 24⅜" (66 × 62 cm)

Rogier van der Weyden, 1399/1400–1464, *Flemish*

BRAQUE TRIPTYCH

THE PERSONALITY OF Rogier van der Weyden dominates mid-fifteenth-century Flemish painting. After working closely with Robert Campin, as shown by his *Annunciation* (also in the Louvre), he developed during his period of maturity a broad and even monumental style, certainly subject to Eyckian realism but still linked to the great Gothic tradition. The refined spiritual pathos that imbues his naturalism likewise remains that of medieval piety. Such a pictorial language had an intense effect on his contemporaries, and his influence throughout Europe was considerable.

The *Braque Triptych* offers a perfect example of his art. "I know no other work in which Rogier expresses himself with such impressive eloquence," wrote the great art historian Max J. Friedländer. It can be dated with some precision around 1451–52. The arms painted on the back of the wings are those of Jehan Braque and his wife, Catherine de Brabant, from Tournai, and it is likely that the triptych had been commissioned from Rogier either on the occasion of their marriage in 1451, or immediately after Braque's early death in 1452. It thus belongs to the period following the artist's trip to Rome (1450), a moment of equilibrium that still shows a desire for clear arrangement, a certain formalism—which his Italian experience could only have encouraged—but henceforth softened by a more refined psychological characterization and an enrichment of color. The picture's excellent state of preservation makes this obvious to us even now.

The triptych, a precious devotional object protected by the closing of its wings, remained in the Braque family until the end of the sixteenth century. It turned up in England in the nineteenth century, and it was purchased by the Louvre in 1913.

Panel (Central panel) 13 × 24⅜" (33 × 62 cm)
(Each wing) 13 × 10⅝" (33 × 27 cm)

Geertgen tot Sint Jans, late fifteenth century, *Flemish*

THE RAISING OF LAZARUS

ALTHOUGH DURING THE fifteenth century Ghent and Bruges, Tournai, and then Brussels were the principal centers of Flemish painting, other towns were also the scenes of significant artistic activity, especially in the northern provinces of the country, the present Netherlands. Examples of such work are today quite scarce due to the iconoclastic destruction that took place in the sixteenth century. It was Haarlem that witnessed the career of the most remarkable of Dutch painters, Geertgen tot Sint Jans, so nicknamed because he worked primarily for the monastery of the Knights of Saint John in that city. We know very little for certain about the life of the artist, said to have died at the age of twenty-eight, probably shortly before 1495; but scholars agree in attributing to him some fifteen paintings, among them *The Raising of Lazarus,* acquired by the Louvre in 1902.

Geertgen's language is the one forged fifty years earlier in Ghent and Bruges, and which he learned during his youth in one of these cities, or else without leaving Haarlem, through his teacher Albert van Ouwater. But he uses it with a quite personal accent, in which some scholars detect a regional flavor already distinctly Dutch. Be that as it may, the very conception of *The Raising of Lazarus* appears strongly original, despite some borrowings of detail from the same subject as painted by Ouwater (Berlin-Dahlem, Gemäldegalerie). Narrative freshness is here combined with a new insistence on form that imparts distinctness to the volumes and plastic simplification. A particular charm issues from this representation of a gathering of devout burghers, while an admirable landscape dotted with trees, turrets, and ponds lends a poetic dimension to the scene.

Panel 50 × 38⅛" (127 × 97 cm)

Quentin Massys (*or* Metsys), 1466–1530, *Flemish*
MONEYCHANGER AND HIS WIFE

FROM OLD TEXTS AND descriptions we know that the great Flemish masters of the fifteenth century, in addition to their portraits and religious pictures, painted scenes recounting everyday life. There is nothing surprising about this, since their art was based on a faithful observation of reality. None of these genre scenes has survived, but the *Arnolfini Wedding* by Jan van Eyck (London, National Gallery), which is a portrait, or the *Saint Eligius* by Petrus Christus (New York, Metropolitan Museum, Lehman Collection), a scene with a religious pretext, may give us some idea.

We know that around 1440 Jan van Eyck painted the half-length figures of a "merchant doing his accounts with an assistant," a painting that has since disappeared, and Quentin Massys was very likely inspired by such a composition to paint *Moneychanger and His Wife,* close to sixty-five years later. The costumes, the characters, the style of the illuminated book through which the wife is leafing, belong moreover to the period of van Eyck, as does the meticulous workmanship shown by the painting. A revealing detail of this return to Eyckian sources is the trompe-l'oeil treatment of the convex mirror in the foreground, reflecting the fourth side of the room and the painter himself. The picture thus constitutes a deliberately archaic homage to the founding fathers of Flemish naturalism, an interpretation which is supported by other paintings of Quentin Massys and his contemporary Gerard David.

The interest of the work nevertheless goes beyond that of a simple "revival." It was itself imitated and copied, serving as a model for numerous Flemish genre scenes of the sixteenth century

The picture may possibly have belonged to Rubens. Mentioned in several seventeenth-century collections, it reappeared in Paris in 1806 and was bought by the Musée Napoléon.

Panel 28 × 26" (71 × 68 cm)

Hieronymus Bosch, 1453?–1516, *Netherlandish*

THE SHIP OF FOOLS

THE SUBJECT OF THIS SMALL PICTURE, the only Bosch in the Louvre, is much debated. It is usually related to the book by Sebastian Brant, *Narrenschiff* ("Ship of Fools"), that appeared in 1494 and deals with the old medieval theme of the "bark of easy livers," developing in a farcical tone a critique of the moral corruption of all members of society. On the other hand, it has been taken to be one wing of a diptych representing the Paradise of Fools. Others have seen it as an illustration of one of the seven deadly sins, Gluttony, or a satire on one of the five senses, Taste. It has also been thought that the work, in which the chief characters are a monk and a nun, constituted a violent attack on the dissolute life of the clergy. There has even been an attempt at a psychoanalytic interpretation by identifying certain erotic symbols. In more general terms, the painting illustrates a theme dear to Bosch, who imparts a moral meaning to all his works—that of human folly neglecting the teachings of Christ.

The lower part of the panel has been cut off: it was once thought that the *Allegory of Gluttony and Lust* in the Yale University Art Gallery in New Haven, similar in style, might be the missing piece, but the idea has now been abandoned. The free and brilliant brushwork, comparable to a sketch, with strokes that revel in effects of impasto and transparency, and the iridescent colors, make it possible to date *The Ship of Fools* around 1490–1500, a little before the *Haywain* in the Prado.

Panel 22 ½ × 12 ¼" (57 × 31 cm)

64

Pieter Bruegel the Elder, 1525/1530–1569, *Flemish*

THE CRIPPLES

DESPITE ITS SMALL SIZE, this is by no means a minor work. Reduced to six characters and a bit of landscape, the composition—constructed with astonishing plastic conciseness and precision—forcefully illustrates the complexity of Bruegel's genius, which dominates Flemish painting of the sixteenth century.

The subject has given rise to several different interpretations. Today it is no longer taken to be a political accusation directed against the Spanish occupation of Flanders, with physical deformity in this case symbolizing moral decrepitude. We should instead see these poor cripples as lepers, who indeed are known to have worn fox tails on their clothes during Carnival. If this explanation is correct, the scene may be taking place in the courtyard of the *lazaretto,* at the moment of departure for Carnival, and the woman at the right would be a nurse. But one should also point out that the fanciful headgear sported by the five wretches (crown, shako, beret, cap, miter) correspond to the various social classes (king, soldier, burgher, peasant, bishop). An allegorical intention thus cannot be ruled out. Whatever the iconographic key to the theme may be, and it remains obscure, Bruegel here creates a powerful image of human misery. Isolated in their misfortune, the cripples detach themselves from each other in accordance with a very remarkable centrifugal motion. The glimpse of landscape, between blank walls in the background of the picture, suffices by its springlike freshness to evoke, in a quite striking contrast, the unblemished health of nature—an inaccessible vista that nevertheless seems to fascinate and perhaps attract the leper seen from the back.

The painting, which may have belonged to Queen Christina of Sweden (coming from the imperial collections in Prague) or, according to other sources, to various seventeenth-century collections in Antwerp, was given to the Louvre in 1892 by the art critic Paul Mantz.

Panel 7⅛ × 8¼" (18 × 21 cm)

Peter Paul Rubens, 1577–1640, *Flemish*

FLEMISH KERMESSE

LIKE BRUEGEL'S PEASANT scenes in the sixteenth century, the *Kermesse* constitutes one of the heights of Flemish genre painting in the seventeenth century. The countryfolk of David Teniers and Adriaen Brouwer are here swept into the vortex of a village fair, with a frenetic but shrewdly calculated rhythm that links the entwined groups in garlands. Such a construction, relying on an inexhaustible play of curves and countercurves in space, gives a stunning demonstration of Baroque dynamism and vitality. At the very moment when he may have felt his strength declining (the work is usually dated around 1635–36), Rubens glorifies the most unbridled carnal appetites. But he manages to give another dimension, that of time, to his great sensual poem: moving from left to right in the composition, the tumult diminishes and loses itself little by little in the peaceful fields.

The *Kermesse* was acquired for Louis XIV from M. de l'Aubespine, Marquis de Hauterive, in 1685. Up until then, despite the presence in the Luxembourg palace of the sumptuous series of monumental canvases devoted to the life of Marie de Médicis and painted by Rubens in 1621–25 (now in the Louvre), French taste, upheld by the official doctrine of the Académie, had remained somewhat backward with regard to Flemish painting. The "Poussinists," still enamored of classicism, set themselves against the "Rubenists," who represented the need for renewal among the younger French painters. The arrival of the *Kermesse* in the royal collections signaled the victory of the Rubenists. From then on Flemish paintings were to enrich French collections in great number, and painters were to profit by the lessons in pictorial freedom and richness of color supplied by these great masters. There is no better example of the fortunate result of this stimulus than Watteau, who copied several groups from the *Kermesse* and probably kept in mind the diminishing cadence of the composition for the *Pilgrimage to the Island of Cythera*.

Panel 58⅝ × 102¾" (149 × 261 cm)

Peter Paul Rubens, 1577–1640, *Flemish*

THE ARRIVAL OF MARIE DE MÉDICIS AT MARSEILLES

QUEEN MARIE DE MÉDICIS, wishing to add painted decorations to her Luxembourg palace in Paris, on which construction began in 1613, turned to Rubens, who was then the most celebrated painter in Europe and had worked for her sister, the Duchess of Mantua. The artist, in Paris at the beginning of 1622, was commissioned to execute two series of pictures to decorate two galleries, one to the glory of Henry IV, Marie's husband, who had been assassinated in 1610, the other to the glory of the queen. She decided to begin with the gallery dedicated to her own person, and the other was never to get beyond the state of rough sketches. The huge undertaking was finished in 1625: the twenty-one large canvases were ready by the time of the marriage of Henriette of France and Charles I of England in May of that year. Later the group of paintings went through a long period of uncertain fame, being shifted about in the Luxembourg, until they were transported to the Louvre in 1816.

Rubens, in order to tell the story—one rather deficient in striking events—of a princess without much character, employs all the resouces of allegorical language with so much verve, robustness, and conviction that he completely wins the spectator's allegiance. In this episode, we see Marie de Médicis, Henri IV's young bride, disembarking at Marseilles in 1600. The galley bears the Medici arms; the queen is welcomed by France and the city of Marseilles; in the air, personified Fame announces the good news of her arrival. In the foreground, Neptune, with Nereids and tritons, moors the boat: the three Nereids, fresh and vigorous, painted from nature and iridescent with pearly light, are among the finest passages in Rubens's work.

The *Life of Marie de Médicis* was to be, from the end of the seventeenth century to the beginning of the twentieth, an inexhaustible source of examples for French artists: all the "colorist" painters came to take lessons from it. We might mention Antoine Coypel and Cézanne, who made drawings precisely from the nymphs in the *Arrival at Marseilles,* and Delacroix, who executed several painted copies of the picture, both of the whole work and of details.

Canvas 155⅛ × 116⅛" (349 × 295 cm)

Anthony van Dyck, 1599–1641, *Flemish*

PORTRAIT OF CHARLES I

IN HIS YOUTH A pupil of, and collaborator with, Rubens, Anthony van Dyck had become, after a long visit to Italy (1621–27), one of the most fashionable painters in Antwerp, the art capital of Flanders. In 1632 he accepted an invitation to come to England, where in the next nine years until his death he had an extremely brilliant career, painting hundreds of portraits of the royal family and the English nobility. The image of listless elegance that he gave the aristocracy was to remain the sometimes tyrannical model for most English portrait painters down to the nineteenth century.

"Principal Painter Ordinary" to the king, who knighted him, van Dyck executed several portraits of the sovereign. The one in the Louvre, painted between 1635 and 1638 (the latter date is that of the payment to the artist), was part of various large French collections in the eighteenth century before entering that of the Comtesse du Barry, last mistress of Louis XV, who claimed to be related to the Stuarts. The work was purchased from her for the royal collections in 1775.

In his various portraits of Charles I, van Dyck depicts him as a soldier or in full regalia. Here he appears as a gentleman returning from the hunt. Despite the absence of any royal attributes, the majesty of the pose unquestionably designates him as the sovereign, the leader of a refined society the fragility of which was to be revealed by history. Embodying a moment in civilization through the simultaneously familiar and poetic evocation of a personality, the work is also a sumptuous piece that set an example for English painters.

Canvas 107⅛ × 83½" (272 × 212 cm)

Jacob Jordaens, 1593–1678, *Flemish*

THE FOUR EVANGELISTS

LIKE VAN DYCK'S *Portrait of Charles I,* this picture was acquired under Louis XVI, in this case in 1784. At that time there was an active concern to enlarge the royal collections, especially with Flemish and Dutch paintings, in order to set up a truly encyclopedic museum representing the various schools of painting.

The Four Evangelists, painted around 1625, is highly representative of Jordaens's early style, often considered the most original in his long career. The compact composition, the presentation of the figures in half length, and the sharp illumination strongly emphasizing the wrinkles of the old men and hollowing the folds of their garments, remind us that in his youth Jordaens, like Rubens, had absorbed the lesson of Caravaggio's art, transmitted by artists returning from Italy, such as Abraham Janssens. He also adheres deeply to the very spirit of Caravaggio by giving his sacred personages the features of common people and expressing thereby an intense and serious religious feeling. But his rich technique and the cordial warmth of his naturalism are distinctly Flemish.

Canvas 52 × 46½" (132 × 118 cm)

Frans Hals, 1580/1585–1666, *Dutch*

LA BOHÉMIENNE

PORTRAITIST OF THE BURGHERS of Haarlem, whom he sometimes assembled in his vast group portraits of guilds, Frans Hals also painted popular types, picturesque figures of the streets and docks, whom he shows in a jovial and disheveled state, winking an eye or bursting with laughter. Indeed, with her daringly low neckline, the "Bohemian girl" must be a prostitute. These character portraits are usually dated around 1627–30, and they are connected, by subject as well as conception, with the Caravaggesque trend imported a few years earlier from Rome to Utrecht by Terbrugghen and Honthorst.

Lifelike and natural, painted in the clear light of day, *La Bohémienne* shines with truth, a spontaneous truth, seized on the wing. This dynamism, typically Baroque, is manifest in the very execution of the painting; the hatchings of the brushwork, applied with inimitable verve, suggest the mobility of life.

La Bohémienne, which belonged in the eighteenth century to the Marquis de Marigny, brother of Madame de Pompadour, is said to have been the first purchase of one of the most amazing collectors of the nineteenth century, Dr. La Caze, who began as a physician for the poor and devoted his life to an exclusive passion, his collection of paintings. Without unusual financial means, he accumulated in his small Paris home nearly six hundred pictures, especially from the seventeenth and eighteenth centuries, bought at auction or from dealers with a flair and a disregard for fashion that brought him countless lucky finds. He owned another masterpiece by Frans Hals, a *Portrait of a Woman,* painted around 1650. At his death in 1869, Dr. La Caze left his whole collection to the museums of France. Slightly more than half of the pictures were distributed to provincial museums; the Louvre kept 272 of them, which probably constitute the most important bequest it has ever received through the generosity of a single private citizen.

Panel 22⅞ × 20½" (58 × 52 cm)

Rembrandt Harmensz van Rijn, 1606–1669, *Dutch*

BATHSHEBA

AT THE TIME HE PAINTED *Bathsheba,* in 1654, Rembrandt was burdened by heavy personal difficulties: a precarious financial situation, and condemnation by the church of Amsterdam for his liaison with Hendrickje Stoffels, who gave birth to their child that same year. But these worries, which were to become still more serious, do not make Rembrandt the "doomed painter" of legend. He was the leader of a school, anxious to leave his mark on his times, and at the height of his technical resources. It was during this period that he created some of his greatest masterpieces, suffused with both humanity and familiar truth, and evincing the historical and moral awareness that a "painter of history" must have. *Bathsheba,* in its moving sincerity, is certainly a "portrait" of Hendrickje shown in an intimate situation. But the composition also relates, with profound simplicity, the biblical episode of Bathsheba surprised at her bath by David. When summoned by a note to come to him, she seems to ponder and hesitate almost painfully before yielding to sin. With a probable ambition to rival the radiant goddesses of the Venetian Renaissance, Rembrandt imparts to the subject a distinct psychological resonance quite alien to those exclusively sensual models: "The miracle of Rembrandt's *Bathsheba,* the naked body permeated with thought, was never repeated." (Kenneth Clark)

The painting entered the Louvre in 1869 with the La Caze Collection, rejoining the Rembrandt masterpieces acquired successively under Louis XIV (*Self-Portrait,* 1660), Louis XV (*The Angel Leaving Tobias,* 1637), Louis XVI (*Supper at Emmaus,* 1648), and Napoleon III (*Slaughtered Ox,* 1655). Since the late seventeenth century and except perhaps during the neoclassical period, the artist's mysterious lighting effects, the resources of his craft, had continued to fascinate French painters and art-lovers. *Bathsheba* elicited a new tone that is at first glance surprising; Eugène Fromentin, a great connoisseur of Dutch masters, actually called it "a rather bizarre study from life."

Canvas 55⅞ × 55⅞" (142 × 142 cm)

Jacob van Ruisdael, 1628/29–1682, *Dutch*

LE COUP DE SOLEIL ("Interval of Sunshine")

THIS CANVAS, ONE OF THE MOST famous Dutch landscapes of the seventeenth century, was bought in 1785 at the Comte de Vaudreuil sale, through which occasion the collections of Louis XVI were augmented by several pictures that today rank among the Flemish and Dutch masterpieces in the Louvre: one might mention the *Portrait of Hélène Fourment and Her Children* by Rubens, the *Four Evangelists* by Jordaens, and the *Portrait of Hendrickje Stoffels* by Rembrandt.

In the seventeenth century, the landscape painters of the northern Low Countries generally took for their subject an actual natural view, executed with a great concern for fidelity and a pious exactitude in the rendering of details. Ruisdael, on the other hand, here depicts an imaginary landscape. He tries, as it were, to sum up nature by showing its various aspects in a downward view within a single composition. The plain, the hills, the mountain, the river, and the manmade structures (town, castle, mill) are integrated in the landscape into which the human figure (bathers, horseman) itself almost merges. By setting this grandiose spectacle before us, he would seem to be insisting on everything that is fleeting and temporary in nature, and perhaps in human life—the passing clouds, the blowing wind, the flowing river, the traveler proceeding on his way, the ray of fugitive sunlight falling for a brief moment on the wheatfield. The feeling of melancholic lyricism that is unique to Ruisdael in his finest works is deeply felt in this painting. This type of synthetic, almost symbolic landscape is related to those of Rembrandt, also strongly human and lyrical; but the light colors, the blue-gray and delicate nuances of green, are far from Rembrandt's warm and golden tones. In this canvas, which has sometimes been dated around 1670–75 (or, more correctly, shortly after 1660), Ruisdael seems to place himself in the ideal and heroic current of Italian landscape; it is the time of his maturity, when he devoted himself largely to grand panoramic views, meadows or beaches with contrasts in light that are both pronounced and subtle.

The delicate and modest melancholy of such paintings, on display at the Louvre in the last century, had a considerable influence on the landscape painters of the Barbizon School, Théodore Rousseau and Jules Dupré.

Canvas 32⅝ × 38⅝" (83 × 98 cm)

Jan Vermeer, 1632–1675, *Dutch*

THE LACEMAKER

THERE ARE FEW MORE striking cases of the caprices of taste than that of Vermeer who, famous in his own day, sank into oblivion for a century and a half, before reemerging in the middle of the nineteenth century, largely because of the research and enthusiasm of the French critic Théophile Thoré. In 1866 he published a study regrouping the artist's works, few in number and several of which had been attributed to other painters. By 1870 the Louvre had bought *The Lacemaker* at the sale of a Dutch collection. Since then, interest in the painter has been keen, and Vermeer has become one of the demigods of our "museum without walls," placed no doubt in an unduly prominent position in relation to other painters of Dutch interiors (Terborch, Metsu, Emmanuel de Witte, or Pieter de Hooch).

The Lacemaker is usually dated around 1664–65, that is, somewhere toward the end of Vermeer's brief career, shortly after, for example, *Woman in Blue* (Amsterdam, Rijksmuseum). The subject evokes a theme that recurs often in his work, that of a woman placed in the lighted seclusion of her home and absorbed in a silent household task (as here), reading a letter, or playing music. Despite its small size, or perhaps because of the concentration of effects that such miniaturization entails, the picture represents the quintessence of Vermeer's art. The absolute objectivity of the scene, which rules out any intellectual or emotional interpretation, is obtained by the pure magic of paint, and this has always earned *The Lacemaker* the enthusiastic admiration of other painters. Renoir saw it as the "most beautiful painting in the Louvre," along with Watteau's *Pilgrimage to the Island of Cythera*.

Panel 9½ × 8¼" (24 × 21 cm)

Pieter de Hooch, 1629–1684?, *Dutch*

THE DRINKER

FOR A LONG TIME much more famous than Vermeer, Pieter de Hooch made it his specialty to depict indoor or outdoor scenes showing unusual individuals in their daily occupations. The happiest time of his career was the period he spent in Delft (1654–c. 1662), corresponding to the years of his maturity and to which this picture, dated 1658, belongs. The strict perspective imparted to the interior of the room and the subtlety of the yellow light that glides over the forms make *The Drinker* a rare masterpiece, organized with all the rigor of a geometer and expressed with all the delicacy of a poet. The emptiness of the foreground, occupied only by the chair and the little sleeping dog, and the row of rooms visible through the center door, are compelling by their almost musical effect, just as we are compelled by the golden range of colors, in which dark surfaces break off, silky white or pearly grays gleam, and the outspoken red of the young woman's skirt blazes in the center. But the concentrated poetry of this silent painting, an almost magical piece of "pure painting," should not deceive us as to the true subject of the picture, which very probably represents a house of assignation: the old woman in the center is the procuress, who has brought together the man in black and the young prostitute in the red skirt, for whom he pours a drink. The playing card on the floor indicates that it is not a respectable house, and the picture hanging to the right, a *Christ and the Woman Taken in Adultery,* probably constitutes a discreet and indirect allusion to the sexual theme of the canvas. The wall map hanging behind the main group, something that Vermeer also frequently included, shows a view of Amsterdam.

The picture, which was donated to the Louvre in 1974 by Mme Piatigorsky, had been in a number of famous collections: the Braamcamp in Amsterdam, the Hope in England, and the Rothschild in Paris.

Canvas 26¾ × 23⅝" (68 × 60 cm)

Master of Saint Bartholomew, Late 15th–early 16th century, *German*

DESCENT FROM THE CROSS

THE LOUVRE OWNS ONE of the finest collections outside Germany of primitive paintings of the School of Cologne, the most important school in the Teutonic countries in the fifteenth century. It does not contain any works by Lochner, the only artist of this school whose name is known, but the Master of the Holy Family, the Master of the Legend of Saint Ursula, and the Master of Saint Séverin are brilliantly represented, the last with two pictures that entered the museum in 1972.

The *Descent from the Cross* by the Master of Saint Bartholomew is the uncontested masterpiece of this group. The altarpiece has been in Paris since the sixteenth century: at that time it was in the Jesuit *maison professe* in the Rue Saint-Antoine; in the eighteenth century it was in the Val-de-Grâce church and was confiscated during the Revolution. The framework of sculpture surrounding the composition shows the tau and bell of Saint Anthony: the work must have been painted for a community of Anthonin monks, perhaps for the abbey of Saint Antoine in Paris. Two poorly preserved panels in the Gemeente Museum in Arnhem were once thought to be the side sections of an altarpiece whose center would have been the picture in the Louvre, but this idea is generally rejected today.

The Master of Saint Bartholomew, perhaps of Netherlandish origin, was active between 1478 and 1510; he was the greatest painter of Cologne in this period when the Gothic style glowed with its final luster before being overtaken by the tendency toward Mannerism. Here the extravagant forms, the twisted gestures, the exacerbated nervousness of the conception are quite typical of this art. The obsession with expressive details, the precious colors, such as the idea of the framework painted on a gold background against which the figures stand out like painted sculptures, evoke the famous *Descent from the Cross* by Van der Weyden (Prado), which serves as a prototype for the painting.

The work can be dated around 1500–1505, at the time of the Munich Pinakothek's *Saint Bartholomew Altarpiece*, which gave its name to the painter.

Panel 86⅝ × 84¼" (220 × 214 cm)

Albrecht Dürer, 1471–1528, *German*

SELF-PORTRAIT

IN THE FIFTEENTH CENTURY, the individual artist gained a new awareness of his own personality, while the new methods of painting, both in Italy and in northern Europe, began to allow for more characterization in the representation of individual faces. First, the painter introduced his own likeness among the personages in his compositions; later, he devoted an entire canvas to it, in the form of an isolated self-portrait, as Jean Fouquet (*Self-Portrait,* enamel, Louvre) was one of the very first to do. The example was followed by most artists from the sixteenth century on.

Dürer, like Rembrandt, subjected his own features to such scrutiny throughout his career. Rooted in individualism, these self-portraits proclaim proud self-knowledge, but also betray the questioning nature of his philosophical temperament. In the first of these self-portraits, the one in the Louvre, the artist is twenty-two years old. He is ending his apprenticeship travels in Germany, before settling down the following year in Nuremberg. Some scholars consider the picture to be an engagement portrait painted for Agnes Frey, whom he was to marry in 1494. The plant he holds in his hand, a sprig of eryngium (or thistle), would thus be a symbol of conjugal fidelity. Others see another allegorical meaning, that of the sufferings of Christ. In any case, the two lines inscribed beside the date (''My affairs go as ordained on high'') demonstrate a Christian intention.

Parchment on canvas 22 × 17⅜" (56 × 44 cm)

Hans Holbein the Younger, 1497/98–1543, *German*
PORTRAIT OF ERASMUS

AFTER LEADING A rather cosmopolitan existence, Erasmus of Rotterdam (c. 1466–1536), in his day perhaps the most illustrious of northern European humanists, settled in Basel. There he became a friend of the painter Holbein, who had been living in that city since 1515. Holbein painted several portraits of Erasmus. The one in the Louvre is generally thought to be the picture that the philosopher himself sent to England in 1523 to his old friend Thomas More, who three years later was to become one of Holbein's principal patrons during the artist's first English sojourn. The painter shows the philosopher writing the opening lines of his *Commentary on the Gospel of Saint Mark.* The representation of a writer at work, a secular derivation from the traditional one of *Saint Jerome in His Study,* was a frequent theme after the fifteenth century. Quentin Massys had already illustrated it in his 1517 *Portrait of Erasmus* (British Royal Collections), and Dürer was to do the same for his engraved portrait of the humanist (1526).

What distinguishes the Louvre portrait from the other likenesses of Erasmus, making it more intense and thus more convincing, is the extreme simplification of the presentation. Renouncing the picturesque element usually provided in this type of portrait by an accumulation of books, Holbein concentrates the viewer's attention on the face and hands. There is no doubt that Erasmus himself was mindful of the image he meant to leave to posterity through his portraits: an image expressing the very idea of intellectual action. Few artists have been as successful as Holbein in giving form to this idea.

The picture comes from the collection of Louis XIV (and before him of Charles I), who owned several other Holbein masterpieces that today are in the Louvre, in particular the portraits of *Archbishop William Warham,* a friend of Erasmus who received another portrait from him (now in Longford Castle in Great Britain), and of *Nicolas Kratzer*—both of which date from the artist's first visit to England (1527–28)—and the *Portrait of Anne of Cleves,* painted for Henry VIII in 1539.

Panel 16½ × 12⅝" (42 × 32 cm)

El Greco, 1541–1614, *Spanish*

CRUCIFIXION WITH TWO DONORS

DOMENIKOS THEOTOKOPOULOS was of Greek origin (he was born in Crete)—hence his nickname—and he was trained in Venice. After a stay in Rome, in 1577 he settled in Toledo, a city with which he has been most nearly identified. His singular art has been restored to first rank by writers and art-lovers of the twentieth century, struck by the "modernism" of his vision, which, in the wake of the great Italian Mannerists, was not afraid to stretch and violently distort the proportions of the body, and to use a simplified and rapid brushwork that left visible strokes in deliberately strange and unrealistic ranges of color.

Like so many other El Greco masterpieces, the *Crucifixion with Two Donors* comes from Toledo, where it adorned the altar of the church of the Hieronymite nuns of the Queen. In the nineteenth century, it was part of King Louis-Philippe's *Galerie Espagnole,* and was bought by the Louvre in 1908. It is almost certainly the earliest *Crucifixion* by El Greco to come down to us. Later this theme recurred frequently in the painter's work, expressed in an increasingly dramatic style, the subject treated with an ever greater freedom of execution, and the anatomical forms tending to dissolve. Here the still "discreet" proportions of the body of Christ, his accurate and carefully molded forms, sculpturally firm, show El Greco to be still close to his Italian teachers. But the upward movement of the body, which seems no longer held to the cross by the three nails and rises like a flame, the three faces with their upraised eyes, and especially the astonishing stormy sky with its broad, violently contrasted stretches and rigorous monochrome—blacks, silvery or ochered whites, bluish grays—are characteristic of the climate of lofty grandeur, of harshness and mysticism of the finest works of Spanish painting.

Canvas 98⅜ × 70⅞ (250 × 180 cm)

Francisco de Zurbarán, 1598–1664, *Spanish*

FUNERAL OF SAINT BONAVENTURE

DURING THE SEVENTEENTH century, the militant piety of the great Spanish monastic orders (Franciscans, Dominicans, Carthusians, Carmelites, Hieronymites) multiplied the number of painting sequences narrating, in several episodes, the life of this or that saint; they were comparable in that respect to the Italian fresco cycles of previous centuries. A good many of these sequences were broken up at the beginning of the nineteenth century, when, as a result of the War of Independence in Spain and later at the time when the government authorized the sale of ecclesiastical property, European collectors and dealers sent out of Spain a great number of pictures, which today represent Spain's "golden age" in museums all over the world. The Louvre thus owns two of the eleven pictures painted by Murillo for the cloister of the Franciscans in Seville (including the famous *Angels' Kitchen*), and four of the eight canvases that adorned the church of the Franciscan Colegio de San Buenaventura in the same city. Two of these paintings are by Francisco de Herrera the Elder, the other two by Zurbarán. They were bought in 1858 from the collection of Marshal Soult and represent the most important group of Spanish paintings assembled in the early nineteenth century before the one established by Louis Philippe.

The *Funeral of Saint Bonaventure* illustrates the final episode in the story of the Franciscan saint, who died in 1274 during the Council of Lyons. The saint's religious brothers are gathered solemnly around his body, along with the great figures present at the Council, Pope Gregory X and Jaime I, king of Aragon. The work dates from 1629. Zurbarán was then established in Seville, one of the centers of "tenebrism," a movement that had inspired the young Velázquez before his departure for Madrid. Its spiritual intensity and simplicity, which connect this lamentation scene with those of the primitives, as well as its severe composition, cut by the unforgettable white diagonal of the corpse, place the painting among Zurbarán's strongest creations during the early part of his career.

Canvas 98⅜ × 88⅝" (250 × 225 cm)

94

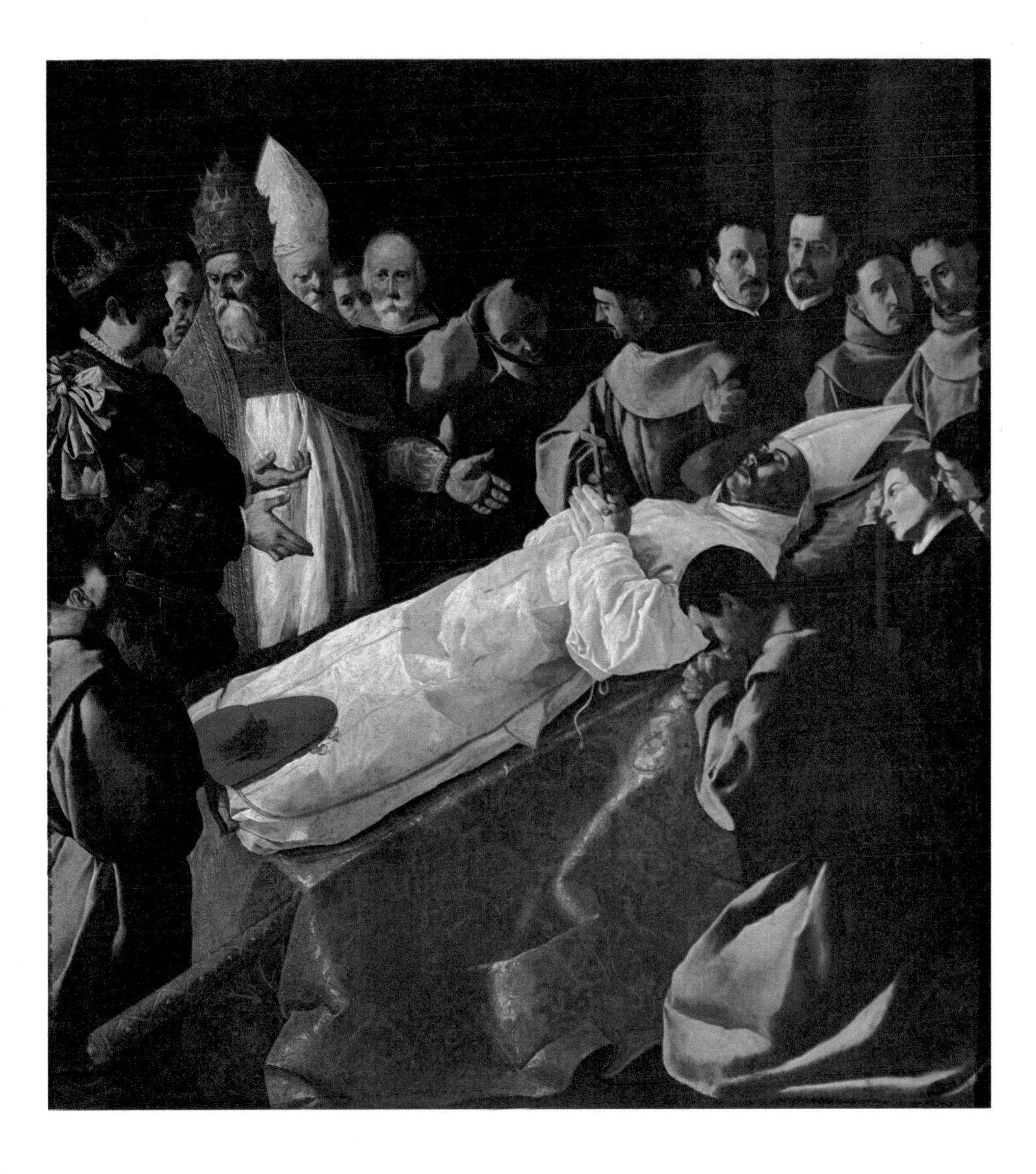

Jusepe Ribera, 1591–1652, *Spanish*
THE ADORATION OF THE SHEPHERDS

ARRIVING AS A VERY YOUNG man in Italy, where because of his short stature, he was nicknamed "Lo Spagnoletto" (the little Spaniard), Ribera, after working for a few years in Rome, in 1616 settled in Naples, a city that he was seldom to leave again. To understand his painting, one should see it as both Spanish, in its taste for a sometimes brutal harshness and in all its aspects of violence and drama, and Italian, for its sense of eloquence, harmony, composition and color, and poetic refinement. His pictures constituted the point of departure for a whole current of painting in Naples; and sent in great numbers to Spain, they had a lasting influence on Spanish artists. The signature of the *Adoration of the Shepherds*—"Jusepe de Ribera español Academico Romano"—proclaims both the painter's loyalty to his native land and his pride in the title received before 1626 in Rome, as a member of the Accademia di San Luca.

Ribera's art, sometimes unbearable in its exaggerated horror, is famous for the pitiless realism of his representations of martyrs and for his insatiable curiosity about human deformity, as shown by his admirable painting *Clubfoot* (1642) also in the Louvre. On the other hand, The *Adoration of the Shepherds,* painted in 1650, shows that at the end of his career Ribera could, when faced with a happy subject, find a relaxed and moderated style of sober grandeur and filled with grace in its treatment of a young mother and a child. The passages of sound and vigorous naturalism, well within the Caravaggio tradition—as in the faces and hands of the old men, the fur of the animals, the wisps of straw in the manger—indicate a concern for tactile veracity in the rendering of materials, depicted in thick, rich paint. These were some of the effects that in the nineteenth century such painters as Ribot, Vollon, and Bonnat were especially to admire in the halls of the Louvre.

This canvas was part of the Neapolitan collection of the Duke della Regina; in 1802 it was given by the king of Naples to the French republic, as an indemnity for pictures taken by Neapolitan troops from the church of San Luigi dei Francesi in Rome.

Canvas 93¾ × 70½" (238 × 179 cm)

Bartolomé Esteban Murillo, 1617–1682, *Spanish*

THE YOUNG BEGGAR

DURING THE FIRST PART of his career, Murillo's style was marked by the tenebrist naturalism illustrated in the works of Zurbarán and Ribera. It was during this period (c. 1650) that he painted *The Young Beggar*. One can compare him here to Velázquez in the vigor of his technique and the sincerity with which he treats the most natural aspects of the life of the people. When later he painted more street urchins and other picaresque subjects, this objectivity was less able to resist the lure of the picturesque.

The work, which was in Córdoba in the early eighteenth century and then belonged to the king of Spain, afterwards turned up in France. It was bought for the royal collection in 1782 from the picture dealer Lebrun, husband of Madame Vigée-Lebrun. This acquisition is important, for it marks the introduction of Spanish painting of the "golden age," then still almost unknown in France, into what was to become the Louvre. Although a few princely collections, in particular that of the Duc d'Orléans, already contained masterpieces by the great Spanish painters, the royal collections included only secondary portraits—acquired through exchanges among the royal families—and the fine *Burning Bush* by Francisco Collantes.

The nineteenth century witnessed a growing taste among French artists and collectors for the masters of seventeenth-century Spanish painting. The display in the Louvre until 1848 of Louis Philippe's prodigious personal collection, which contained hundreds of major Spanish works, was to exercise a decisive influence on numerous artists then seeking an escape from Romanticism or academicism in order to rediscover a less conventional, if not less dramatic, vision of reality. At the same time, *The Young Beggar* furnished Courbet, and later Manet and Monet, with an example of truth and pictorial freedom that they were never to forget.

Canvas 53⅞ × 45¼" (137 × 115 cm)

Francisco de Goya, 1746–1828, *Spanish*

PORTRAIT OF CONDESA DEL CARPIO
MARQUESA DE LA SOLANA

IN GOYA'S IMMENSE oeuvre, wherein he practices all genres and explores the most diverse worlds, both as a relentless observer of everyday peculiarities and an often hallucinating poet of the imagination, the portrait holds an essential place throughout his career. The Louvre owns five first-class examples—there are few such remarkable ensembles outside the Prado—among which two portraits of women stand out: that of the *Marquesa de Santa Cruz,* acquired only recently, and that of the *Condesa del Carpio,* more often known as *La Solana,* from the title accorded to her husband in 1795. The exact date of the picture is unknown. We do know that the Condesa del Carpio died in November 1795. Was the portrait painted shortly before this date, as is generally supposed? Or was it done three or four years earlier, before the artist's tragic illness in 1792, which was to bring on his deafness and interrupt his work for some time? In any case, it is related to a group of portraits of standing women, painted during the last five years of the century. These include the *Duchess of Alba,* the painter's mistress (Madrid, Alba Collection; New York, Hispanic Society), and the actress *La Tirana* (Madrid, Academia). These portraits show Goya to be the heir of Velázquez by their masterly simplicity of presentation and the subtlety of their color harmonies—here, grays and blacks orchestrated by a single color, the pink of the headdress.

The portrait is part of a collection that contains mostly portraits (by, among others, the Master of Moulins, van Dyck, David, Ingres, Lawrence, and Drouais), all of exceptional quality. This collection was given to the Louvre by Carlos de Beistegui, a Mexican collector living in France, who in 1942 chose to make this gift as proof of confidence in his adopted country at one of the darkest hours in its history.

Canvas 71¼ × 48" (181 × 122 cm)

Thomas Gainsborough, 1727–1788, *English*

PORTRAIT OF LADY ALSTON

ENGLISH PAINTING IS NOT WELL represented in French museums. The collection in the Louvre was established fairly recently, at the end of the nineteenth century and in the twentieth, and a systematic effort to augment it is still being pursued today. Works by Turner, Fuseli, Wright of Derby, and Zoffany have only now entered the halls of the museum. The Louvre's English collection, despite its small size, is perhaps today the most representative that any museum can show, except of course for those in Great Britain and the United States, which are without rivals in this field.

The *Portrait of Lady Alston,* given to the Louvre in 1947 by the heirs of Baron de Rothschild, belongs to that portion of Gainsborough's career known as his Bath period. In 1759 the painter settled in this elegant health resort, frequented at the time by the most fashionable clientele, and remained there until 1774. There he painted the select and refined society of Bath, frankly orienting his career toward the society portrait. Lady Alston, née Gertrude Durnford (1732–1807), was the wife of Sir Rowland Alston, sixth and last baronet of that name. The Louvre picture is a fine illustration of Gainsborough's Bath style. This style of large aristocratic portrait, in which the model, shown standing and placed against a landscape, looks both dreamy and unconcerned, derives from van Dyck and remained dear to the English school. The shimmering fabrics, the shadowed foliage, and the melancholy and "pre Romantic" air of the portrait, which dates from around 1765, have often caused it to be compared to its contemporary *Viscountess Howe* (Kenwood Castle, near London), painted in a brighter range of pink tones.

Canvas 88⅝ × 65" (225 × 165 cm)

James Abbott McNeill Whistler, 1834–1903, *American*
PORTRAIT OF THE ARTIST'S MOTHER

IN 1871, WHISTLER PAINTED the portrait of his mother, a subject he had been thinking about since 1867. Admitted by a hair's-breadth to the exhibition of the Royal Academy in 1872, the picture had a poor reception. But with this portrait and two or three others that followed—particularly *Thomas Carlyle* (1872–73, Glasgow Art Museum) and *Miss Cecily Alexander* (1872–74, London, Tate Gallery)—the artist revealed a maturity and an equilibrium regained after a period of personal difficulties and aesthetic uncertainties. His recourse to the stimulating example of Velázquez, master of grays, whites, and blacks, is likewise felt in this group of works; significantly, the subtitle of *Portrait of the Artist's Mother* is *Arrangement in Gray and Black, No. 1* (just as the subtitle of the portrait *Thomas Carlyle* is *Arrangement in Gray and Black, No. 2*).

Whistler attached great value to this picture, which went on to become his most popular work. He exhibited it in Philadelphia in 1881, and in Paris at the Salon of 1883. In 1891, thanks to the efforts of a group of friends and admirers, among them Mallarmé and Clemenceau, the painting was bought by the state for the Luxembourg museum. Thus the international renown of a painter hitherto highly controversial in official circles in London and the United States was finally affirmed. The following year Whistler left London to resettle in Paris, where he had worked during his youth in close contact with the circle of "modern" artists (Fantin-Latour, Courbet, Manet) who were leading the way toward Impressionism.

Admired by Degas, the *Portrait of the Artist's Mother* also won the approval of younger men. J.-K. Huysmans, a naturalistic novelist connected with the new Symbolist movement, wrote: "The harmony of gray and India ink black was a joy for eyes surprised by these skillful and profound harmonies. This was realistic painting, wholly intimate, but already extending beyond dreams."

Canvas 57⅛ × 64⅝" (145 × 164 cm)

Jean Malouel, (attr.), Early 15th century, *French*
PIETÀ

PICTURES BY FRENCH "primitive" painters are very rare. There are two reasons for this scarcity: the destruction of much of their work during the Revolution, and the late date—the beginning of our century—at which their originality and interest were recognized, at a time when fifteenth-century Italian and Flemish pictures had already been admired, collected, and studied. The Louvre has the good fortune to own a very representative collection of these works.

At the very end of the fourteenth century and beginning of the fifteenth, the two principal artistic centers were Paris and Dijon, whose painters were among the most brilliant practitioners of the delicate and refined International Gothic style, which was then flourishing in Europe. The *Pietà*, one of the finest examples of this manner (sometimes still called the "Franco-Flemish style"), presents an unusual iconography combining two themes: that of the Christ of Sorrows accompanied by the Virgin and Saint John, and that of the Holy Trinity. The picture, which bears the arms of Burgundy on the back, was painted for Philip the Bold, Duke of Burgundy (1363–1404), and was very likely conceived for the abbey of Champmol in Dijon, built by the dukes to house their tombs and dedicated to the Holy Trinity.

The attribution of this moving work to Jean Malouel, an artist originally from La Gueldre and uncle of the Limbourg brothers, and who in 1397 became court painter to the duke of Burgundy, is very convincing. The elegant and sinuous drawing, the supple modeling, the refined colors are all related to the *Saint Denis Altarpiece* in the Louvre, painted for the Charterhouse of Champmol, finished in 1416 by Henri Bellechose, but very likely designed by Malouel. It would seem that in this work, painted around 1400, the painter was especially influenced by Italian works, such as those of Simone Martini.

Panel diameter 20½" (52 cm)

Jean Fouquet, 1420–1477/81, *French*

PORTRAIT OF CHARLES VII

LIKE THOSE OF OTHER COUNTRIES, the French primitives were long forgotten. They were only rediscovered after the Italians and Flemish in the late nineteenth century. Most of the fifteenth-century French paintings that exist today—and they are rare—had lost their identities and been attributed to other schools. It is significant that Fouquet's *Portrait of Charles VII* had been purchased in 1838 as the work of an unknown "Greek" painter! Its attribution to the greatest French painter of the fifteenth century, who made his career in Tours and worked for the king of France and various members of the court, is nevertheless certain. It is the earliest of his known works, and it was probably painted before the trip he made to Italy around 1445–46.

The work displays both a realism in the interpretation of portraiture that is Flemish in origin, and a simplifying authority in the plastic definition of volumes in which the tradition of French Gothic statuary can perhaps be seen. This original synthesis between two opposing tendencies, naturalism and stylization, was later to be reinforced when the Italian Renaissance furnished the artist with the example of more rational arrangements. It gives the *Portrait of Charles VII* its singularity: an unsparing portrait of the king who was placed on the throne by Joan of Arc as he appears, sickly and sullen, at the window of his oratory in the Sainte-Chapelle of Bourges (from which the picture very likely comes), and at the same time a majestic image of the "*très victorieux roy de France*," as the inscription on the frame designates him.

Panel 33½ × 27⅝" (85 × 70 cm)

Enguerrand Quarton (or CHARONTON), mid-fifteenth century, *French*

PIETÀ OF VILLENEUVE-LÈS-AVIGNON

WHEN IN 1904 a large exhibition held in Paris finally demonstrated the importance of the long misunderstood French primitives, the major revelation was the *Pietà of Villeneuve-lès-Avignon,* which became famous overnight. The Société des Amis du Louvre was able to buy it in 1905 from the town of Villeneuve and offer it to the Louvre.

Having emerged from the shadows, the painting continued to be a mystery for some time. To whom was one to assign this masterpiece of fifteenth-century European painting, for which there was no signature or document to designate the artist? To a Spanish or Portuguese painter, as certain critics thought for a while? Or else to a painter working on the spot in Provence? It is this second hypothesis that deserves to be taken seriously, when one considers that the *Pietà,* far from being an isolated work, is the supreme expression of an actual school, the School of Avignon, the chief center, along with the School of Touraine, of fifteenth-century French painting.

Plastic synthesis of volumes, underscored by strongly contrasting light; monumental strength of composition, recalling great Gothic sculpture; severity of expression—these striking features of the *Pietà* are found in varying degrees in other paintings of the School of Avignon, from the Master of the Annunciation of Aix (c. 1443–45) to Josse Lieffrinxe at the beginning of the sixteenth century. Almost all of these artists came from elsewhere, drawn to Provence by the prosperity that the Hundred Years' War had denied the rest of France. It is the unique mixture of French, Flemish, and Mediterranean influences to which these artists became subject that is responsible for the distinctiveness of the Provençal style.

One painter dominates the School of Avignon in the middle of the fifteenth century (documents mention him in Provence from 1444 to 1466): Enguerrand Quarton, who painted the famous *Coronation of the Virgin* at Villeneuve-lès-Avignon (1453–54). Everything suggests that he was also responsible for the *Pietà of Villeneuve-lès-Avignon.*

Panel 64⅛ × 85⅞" (163 × 218 cm)

Master of Moulins, active c. 1480–1500, *French*

SAINT MARY MAGDALEN AND A FEMALE DONOR

THE GREATEST FRENCH PAINTER of the end of the fifteenth century has been called the "Master of Moulins," from the name of his masterpiece, the great triptych for the collegiate church in Moulins, showing the *Virgin in Glory* worshipped by *Pierre II of Bourbon* and *Anne of France* (1498), around which have been grouped some fifteen works that can be dated between 1480 and 1500.

The Louvre picture, which dates from around 1490, probably constitutes the left section of a triptych whose center section, probably a *Virgin and Child,* and right section, a donor, have been lost. It has been convincingly suggested that this woman donor may be Madeleine of Burgundy, Lady of Laage.

This is one of the finest pictures in the painter's oeuvre, and it shows that the elements, primarily northern, of his style—the taste for naturalism in portraits and the rendering of materials—are closely related to the art of Hugo van der Goes. But the synthetic forms, the calm authority of the volumes, the aristocratic and refined grace are definitely French features, acquired in the Loire region and in central France. The precious delicacy of the modeling, the richness of color, the modest, almost timid reserve of the facial expressions demonstrate this double aspect.

There have been attempts to identify the Master of Moulins: without sufficient proof as Jean Perréal; wrongly as Jean Prévost. The most recent hypothesis, a persuasive one, suggests that he may have been Jean Hey, an artist of Netherlandish origin who painted an *Ecce Homo* (1494, Brussels museum) in a style completely resembling that of the works attributed to the anonymous master.

Panel 22⅞ × 15¾" (58 × 40 cm)

François Clouet, c. 1485–1572, *French*
PORTRAIT OF PIERRE QUTHE

THE ITALIANS ROSSO AND PRIMATICCO, who had been summoned to France by Francis I, led the painters of the School of Fontainebleau frequently to choose mythological subjects for their paintings. But these sixteenth-century French painters still worked primarily in the field of portraiture, thus remaining faithful to the taste for the scrupulous study of individual faces that had been alive in France since the fourteenth century.

Authenticated works by François Clouet are rare. This picture is the only one, except for *Diane de Poitiers* in the National Gallery in Washington, to be signed: the Latin inscription, very complete, bears, in addition to the signature, the name of the sitter, his age, and the date 1562. We thus know with certainty the sitter's identity: Pierre Quthe (1519–after 1568) was a friend of the painter and his neighbor in Paris. An apothecary, he owned a well-known garden of medicinal plants, alluded to here by the open herbal.

François Clouet worked in the vein set forth by his father, Jean, whom he succeeded as court painter in 1541 (like him, he was nicknamed Janet). The face is seen in three-quarters view, the same pose as the sitters in the very numerous pencil drawings left by the two Clouets. The Italian influence is obvious in the *Portrait of Pierre Quthe;* Clouet shows himself to have perhaps been influenced by some of the Italian Mannerists. The attitude, elegant but somewhat fixed, the ivory flesh tones, the cold colors and transparent light, such a detail as the curtain of shiny blue-green material, make one think of portraits by Pontormo, Bronzino, or Salviati. But one is also reminded of such North Italian painters as Giovanni Battista Moroni, or an Italianized Fleming like Antonio Moro (Anthonis Mor). In the middle of the sixteenth century, this type of soberly realistic portrait, the reflection of a placid and benevolent humanism, is truly "European."

Panel 35⅞ × 27⅝" (91 × 70 cm)

Georges de La Tour, 1593–1652, *French*

LE TRICHEUR ("The Cheat")

LIKE VERMEER, GEORGES DE LA TOUR had disappeared from the history of art. He only regained his place some sixty years ago, when several paintings of night scenes illuminated by candlelight were associated with works signed with the then unknown name of Georges de La Tour, thereby showing their author to have been one of the masters of European painting deriving from Caravaggio. Historical research has since been able to tell us something of the life of the artist, who lived in Lunéville in Lorraine, and to reconstitute his oeuvre: some thirty originals and a number of other compositions known only through copies. Corresponding to the taste of our times, his daring geometric simplification, which some have compared to cubism, and the unusual poetry of his inspiration explain why after three centuries of oblivion he has become one of the most popular of French painters.

La Tour's works include night scenes, generally with religious themes (in the Louvre, *The Adoration of the Shepherds, Saint Joseph the Carpenter,* and *The Repentant Magdalen*), and daylight scenes from the Caravaggio repertoire. An example of the latter is *Le Tricheur,* acquired by the Louvre at the end of the great Georges de La Tour exhibition held in Paris in 1972. To such themes as brothels, gambling dens, and cardsharps, which Caravaggio and several of his followers had treated, La Tour gives a moral twist. A young fool is subject to the triple temptation of gambling, wine, and lust; and cynical cleverness will triumph over innocence. It is a disturbing comedy, and La Tour conveys it by the fascinating play of looks and the silent ballet of hands, in one of the most masterfully constructed and subtly painted of all his works.

Canvas 41 ¾ × 57½" (106 × 146 cm)

116

Antoine Le Nain, c.1588–1648, *French*
Louis Le Nain, c.1593–1648

PEASANT FAMILY

A RECENT EXHIBITION IN PARIS gathered together almost all the known canvases by the Le Nain brothers, Antoine, Louis, and Mathieu—a few religious and mythological pictures, some portraits, and above all, the scenes of rural or town life that brought success to the three and inspired numerous imitations. Bringing these works together made it possible to discern more clearly their uneven quality, with the incomparable qualities of one group of paintings, about twenty, standing out by contrast. These show motionless peasants in the Champagne countryside or inside their houses, their gestures as though suspended, their gaze fixed intently on the spectator. The simplicity of composition, often in low relief, and sobriety of color—browns and grays enlivened only by a few more vivid touches—give these pictures the classical severity of the great French masters of the time.

The *Peasant Family* proved to be the strongest and most moving of this group; a reflection of a universal kind on the human condition is expressed here through the image of a simple family partaking of the sacraments of a glass of wine and a loaf of bread. To which of the Le Nain brothers should one attribute such depth and also such pictorial mastery? The artist was long thought to be Louis, but recent study throws doubt on this identification, and no canvas is signed with the first name of any of the brothers. Although for other works, less exceptional and more composite ones, the hypothesis of collaboration cannot be ruled out, here one feels the mind and hand of a single painter. Louis or Antoine? The troublesome enigma has yet to be resolved.

Canvas 44½ × 62⅝" (113 × 159 cm)

Nicolas Poussin, 1594–1665, *French*

THE POET'S INSPIRATION

IN THE INCOMPARABLE COLLECTION of Poussins owned by the Louvre (thirty-eight canvases), *The Poet's Inspiration* is one of the finest and most mysterious. It formed part of the Paris collection of Cardinal Mazarin, where it was admired by Bernini during his visit to France in 1665; later it passed into various English collections and was acquired by the Louvre in 1911.

What does this picture represent? A young man, on the right, crowned by a *putto*, writes under the dictation of Apollo, seated in the center; to the left stands Calliope, the muse of epic poetry. Several books lie on the ground: the *Iliad*, the *Odyssey*, the *Aeneid*. The picture might have been painted in honor of a contemporary poet, or one who had recently died, but the features of the young man are not those of any of the poets admired by Poussin—Ariosto, Tasso, or Marino. The most generally accepted hypothesis claims the poet to be Virgil; the face does in fact resemble the one found on the frontispiece engraved by Claude Mellan from Poussin for an edition of Virgil's works, published in 1641 in Paris by the Imprimerie Royale.

When should the work be dated? Probably around 1630, but in any case well before 1641–42, the date of Poussin's stay in Paris; he was a Norman who became a Roman by adoption. The warm and golden colors and the abundance of massive figures with rounded modeling still belong, in fact, to the "Titian-esque" vein of the painter's work, characteristic of his first years in Rome. The influence of ancient sculpture also appears here strongly, especially in the figure of the Muse; the figure of Apollo is inspired both by antiquity (the *Ares Ludovisi* statue) and by Raphael (fresco of *Apollo and Marsyas* in the Stanza della Segnatura in the Vatican).

Canvas 71⅝ × 83⅞" (182 × 213 cm)

Nicolas Poussin, 1594–1665, *French*

AUTUMN

AT THE END OF HIS LIFE, Nicolas Poussin painted what is probably his artistic testament, the *Four Seasons*. Executed for the Duc de Richelieu, the pictures were finished in 1664 and in the following year, the year of the artist's death, passed into the collection of Louis XIV.

Poussin chose a biblical episode to represent each of the seasons—the Garden of Eden for spring, Ruth and Boaz for summer, the fabulous harvests of the Promised Land for autumn, the Deluge for winter—in accordance with a symbolism that can also give rise to a Christian interpretation of the theme (for autumn, the eucharistic significance of the grape) and probably also a mythological one (here, Bacchus, god of wine). More generally, the *Seasons* constitute the fruit of a long meditation on the stages of human life, which unites certain ancient and Christian philosophical ideas, and incorporates themes relating to the fertility of nature and the destiny of man that Poussin treated throughout his life.

These thoughts had been expressed particularly during the last twenty years of the artist's career by a series of admirable landscapes, masterpieces of classical European landscape, of which the *Seasons* are the supreme accomplishment. There is nothing abstruse in these paintings, despite the complexity of their intellectual and moral implications, but rather a truly pictorial vision of the world, the fervent reconstruction of an ideal—to the extent that it combines all aspects of nature, whether wild or cultivated—and profoundly real countryside.

Canvas 46⅛ × 63" (117 × 160 cm)

Claude Lorrain (CLAUDE GELLÉE), 1600–1682, *French*
CLEOPATRA DISEMBARKING AT TARSUS

THE SEAPORT THEME—ancient palaces and ships framing a glittering sea—is one of Claude Lorrain's favorite subjects, one that brought him success and a long posthumous fame. Turner, as we know, was directly inspired by him and asked in his will that, as a supreme honor, one of his own compositions painted in homage to Claude be hung in the National Gallery, alongside one of the seaport pictures he had admired.

For Claude, the true subject of the picture is the light of the sun, which is reflected in the sea. It brightens the façades of the palaces, and steals across the rigging of the ships. The skillful distribution of masses and the treatment of light (the composition here rests on the marked contrast between an area of shadow and backlighting at the left and the luminosity of the right-hand side) confirm Claude's fundamental classicism and his lyrical idealism, in the line of Bolognese landscape painting and Poussin. But he is, on the other hand, the heir of Elsheimer, Paul Bril, and other early seventeenth-century Northern landscape painters who found in the Roman Campagna a subject of true poetry. Claude achieves a masterful fusion of this twin tradition.

Claude here shows Cleopatra disembarking at Tarsus to meet Mark Antony, whom her hunger for power will lead her to seduce. It is a subject illustrating ambition, to which is contrasted, in the painting's companion piece, *David Crowned by Saul* (also in the Louvre), a scene evoking humility. Without burdening his landscapes with intellectual meanings, as Poussin does, Claude manages to give an atmospheric tonality to each of the two compositions: warm colors for *Cleopatra;* clear, fresh tints for *David*. The two pictures were probably painted in 1642 or 1643 for one of Claude's Roman patrons, Cardinal Giorio, an intimate of Pope Urban VIII. They were purchased for the collection of Louis XIV and kept for a long time in the Grand Trianon at Versailles.

Canvas 46⅞ × 57⅞" (119 × 147 cm)

Philippe de Champaigne, 1602–1672, *French*

EX-VOTO OF 1662

THE DAUGHTER OF Philippe de Champaigne—a painter whose life and career were dominated by the influence of the Jansenist movement—became a nun after 1657, under the name of Soeur Catherine de Sainte Suzanne, in the Paris convent of Port Royal, the center of Jansenism. She fell gravely ill and in 1660 was paralyzed in her legs. Following prayers offered by Mère Catherine-Agnès Arnauld, the young nun was miraculously cured in January 1662 and recovered the use of her legs. Painted immediately afterward by her father as an expression of gratitude and presented by him to the convent, this picture was withdrawn from Port-Royal during the period in which the Jansenists were under attack. It was returned there around 1723, and reached the Louvre when Church property was seized at the time of the Revolution.

Having decided to represent the two nuns kneeling on each side of a crucifix, Philippe de Champaigne chose to show the moment of inner illumination experienced by the two women, the actual moment of the miracle, when Mère Agnès receives the revelation of the approaching recovery. Philippe de Champaigne's knowing art has often been commented on: his "art of suggesting the most while saying the least" (Gide), where a Baroque painter would have depicted clouds, angels, and ecstatic expressions. Here all is sober and severe, almost without color, like the image of the convent cell; the miracle is suggested only by the expressions of the two faces, the old woman's and the very young girl's—motionless faces that express the radiance of the mystical life. The canvas represents the synthesis of the art of the painter as portraitist and religious artist. The concern for realism, pushed sometimes to the point of trompe-l'oeil, betrays Champaigne's Flemish origin, but it is transformed by a psychologist's concern to analyze individuals and a Christian fervor to reveal the workings of the soul.

Canvas 65 × 90⅛" (165 × 229 cm)

Charles Le Brun, 1619–1690, *French*

CHANCELLOR SÉGUIER

CHARLES LE BRUN OWES his fame primarily to his monumental decorations for the palace of Versailles and to the huge historical and allegorical canvases and tapestries that, beginning in 1661, he conceived for the king. Head of a vast collective artistic enterprise, he was indeed the principal inventor of the "grand manner," which marked the reign of Louis XIV and was to spread all over Europe. But one should remember that, for Le Brun, this period of achievement in the service of the king was preceded by twenty years of effort during which the artist little by little gave proof of the extent of his resources and perfected the style that was to triumph at Versailles.

The portrait of *Chancellor Séguier,* the artist's chief patron from the start, is probably the masterpiece of this early period. Painted around 1655–57, it illustrates perfectly the components of Le Brun's art: a fundamental classicism, in the line of Poussin, which imposes on the composition the processional structure of an ancient frieze, without superfluous decoration; the lesson of Roman Baroque, which diversifies the poses of the pages and quickens the rhythm of their steps; and a faithfulness to reality that gives life and physical presence to the figures. One should note that the presentation of this portrait, unique in Le Brun's oeuvre, is highly unusual. Pierre Séguier, chancellor of France, is shown with a pomp unusual for a civil personage, probably to underscore the importance of his functions after the political turmoil of the Fronde.

Canvas 116⅛ × 138¼" (295 × 351 cm)

Antoine Watteau, 1684–1721, *French*

PILGRIMAGE TO THE ISLAND OF CYTHERA

FROM THE MIDDLE OF THE seventeenth century to the end of the eighteenth, French artistic life was largely controlled by the Académie Royale de Peinture et de Sculpture. A painter who did not belong to it could hope for little true success. To be accepted as a member of this academy, one had to send a work painted expressly for this purpose, like the chefs-d'oeuvre of the old medieval guilds. In order to be received by the Académie, Watteau painted the *Pilgrimage to the Island of Cythera* (1717). His colleagues, aware of his independence, had left him free to choose his subject, and the one that he treated did not, in fact, have anything in common with the pompous historical paintings of the other academicians, still for the most part under the sway of the Versailles "grand manner." With Watteau, a new pictorial sensibility was born; it was one that colored the whole eighteenth century until the triumph of neoclassicism.

Here it is no longer a question of a mythological allegory on the theme of Love, nor of the prosaic illustration of some light theatrical piece (the theme of pilgrims to the Island of Love occurs in several ballets and operas of the early eighteenth century), but of a poetic evocation, impalpable as a dream and yet precise in its accurate psychological definition of the various phases in the dialogue between lovers. This composition, the most famous of Watteau's *fêtes galantes,* has long been known as the *Embarkation for Cythera*. But if one rereads the title given to the picture at the time of its reception by the Académie, *Pilgrimage to the Island of Cythera,* one must see it instead as just the opposite, the departure of the lovers from the island of Cythera, a nostalgic theme that is in accord with what we know of Watteau's temperament, and which suggests the flight of time, the brevity and perhaps the illusions of love.

For all the originality of his style and novelty of his poetry, Watteau here demonstrates what he owes to the example of Rubens, to his memory of the Venetians, and even, in the mountain landscape, to Leonardo da Vinci.

Canvas 50⅜ × 76" (128 × 193 cm)

Jean-Baptiste-Siméon Chardin, 1699–1779, *French*

LA POURVOYEUSE ("Back from the Market")

A PAINTER OF STILL LIFES—the greatest of the eighteenth century—Chardin also executed several paintings of figures, delicate representations of childhood, as well as family scenes small in size and showing minor episodes in everyday life. Two of these pictures, the *Industrious Mother* and *Saying Grace,* were presented to Louis XV in 1740 and are now in the Louvre; *La Pourvoyeuse* dates from 1739. It was primarily around these years, while his output of still lifes was somewhat less abundant, that Chardin painted these familiar scenes, returning several times to the same subject. There are thus two other versions of *La Pourvoyeuse*, one (1738) in the Berlin-Dahlem museum, the other (1739) in the National Gallery in Ottawa.

With these simple and serious paintings of domestic life, Chardin recaptures the warmth and sincerity of the Le Nain brothers, in accordance with a tradition that continues on into the nineteenth century with the work of Corot (in some of his human figures) and especially of Millet.

Moved by the silent presence of things ("One makes use of colors, but one paints with feeling," he said), he employed a highly original pictorial language—one that surprised his contemporaries. One of them wrote in this regard: "His way of painting is odd. He places his colors one after another, in such a way that his work somewhat resembles a mosaic of inlaid pieces." Might not Cézanne's method be more or less described this way?

La Pourvoyeuse was acquired by the Louvre in 1867, when the painters of the eighteenth century were regaining their glory after long neglect. It was also the moment of the reemergence of Vermeer.

Canvas 18½ × 14⅝" (47 × 37 cm)

François Boucher, 1703–1770, *French*

BREAKFAST

PAINTED IN THE SAME YEAR (1739) as *La Pourvoyeuse,* and likewise evoking a scene from domestic life, *Breakfast* illustrates quite another aspect of French painting under Louis XV. Here it is a very elegant interior that is shown. Everything—the curved moldings of the pier glass, gilded bronze clock, small table with red lacquer top, console with curved base, silver plate, even the smiling little Chinese figure on the étagère—is in the latest fashion. They represent the triumph of the Rococo style—that overall style that leaves its mark on all forms and utilizes all techniques, answering by its elegance and refinement to the needs of a society given over to luxury and pleasure. Boucher is precisely the painter who best embodies this style. His decorative facility, a pleasant sensuality, and solid pictorial craftsmanship impart to his courtly mythological subjects, pastoral scenes, and landscapes a pliancy and lightness that marvelously harmonize with the arabesques of Rococo decoration. Many of these pictures were, moreover, designed to go with the wood paneling.

At the time he painted *Breakfast,* Boucher had begun an extremely brilliant and fruitful career, working for the king at Versailles and Fontainebleau. He decorated the mansions of the Parisian nobility, designed stage sets for the Opéra and tapestries, and turned out easel paintings and drawings that were snapped up by collectors. Within this immense output, *Breakfast,* though entirely characteristic of his style of painting, constitutes an exception, less for its subject—his work includes other family scenes—than for the tone of intimacy with which this picture of family happiness is treated, and which has led some critics to suppose that the artist has here depicted his young wife and their first two children.

Breakfast was bequeathed to the Louvre in 1894 by Dr. Malécot.

Canvas 31⅞ × 25⅝" (81 × 65 cm)

Jean-Honoré Fragonard, 1732–1806, *French*

BATHERS

"THESE ARE LIVING, vital, sun-drenched bodies, bodies on which the brush places the pure unmixed colors of vermilion, Prussian blue, and chrome yellow to render the light, shadow, and reflection of an arm . . . bodies whose skin the painter half pierces with the reds, browns, and greens of the flayed anatomical figure, with everything that lies beneath the surface of life." These words by the Goncourt brothers (1865), writers who more than anyone else helped to rehabilitate Fragonard after long neglect, glorify the pictorial qualities displayed by the *Bathers*—and we do indeed have here a sparkling bouquet of colors. But they also suggest no less correctly that it was only the painter's sensual appetites and vitality that made it possible for him to bring to life a subject frequently treated by his master Boucher and his rivals, but which had too often become a pretext for agreeable decorative or erotic nonsense.

It is difficult to date the *Bathers* with any certainty. It is usually placed during the period following Fragonard's return from Italy (1761), a time when he was still sensitive to the teachings of Boucher, and when his quick strokes expressed most spiritedly a truly Baroque lyricism and dynamism. The example of Rubens—here one thinks of the fleshy nereids of *Marie de Médicis Disembarking at Marseilles,* which Fragonard saw in the Galerie Médicis in the Luxembourg palace—was probably not far from his mind.

The *Bathers* entered the Louvre in 1869 with the La Caze Collection, which contained eight other canvases by the artist, including four of the stunning *Figures of Fantasy,* as well as an incomparable selection of masterpieces by other great eighteenth-century masters (among them Watteau's *Gilles* and fifteen Chardins), collected by La Caze when they were still out of fashion.

Canvas 25¼ × 31⅞" (64 × 81 cm)

Jacques-Louis David, 1748–1825, *French*

THE SABINE WOMEN

A MILITANT ARTIST, David had taken an active part in the Revolution. After the reaction following the fall of Robespierre in 1794, he had to pay for his commitment by several months in prison. It was there that he conceived the idea for *The Sabine Women*. The huge canvas was finished in 1799. His previous large compositions, the *Oath of the Horatii* (1784) and *Brutus* (1789), had exalted republican virtues. The theme of *The Sabine Women* (the battle of Romans and Sabines at the foot of the Capitol, interrupted by the intervention of Hersilia, a Sabine woman turned Roman) included a more precise political purpose. After the fratricidal struggles of the Revolution, David was urging the French to national reconciliation.

Fifteen years after the *Horatii,* manifesto of the new European historical painting, David proves with *The Sabine Women* that he remains the leader of neoclassicism. Faithful to his principles—heroic nudity, composition in low relief—as well as to his admiration for Poussin, he still seeks to refine his style by renouncing the Roman influence, in order, as he put it, "to restore art to the principles that were followed by the Greeks." This is a concern for stylistic perfection that, very fortunately, does nothing to impair his love of reality, any more than it deprives his craftsmanship of flavor. Better still, his "return to the Greeks" leads him to lighten his palette and to compose an admirable symphony of whites and light tones, unusual harmonies that reappear in the more important portraits of this period (*Madame Récamier,* Louvre; *Madame de Pastoret,* Chicago, Art Institute).

The canvas was exhibited by David in a hall of the Louvre from 1799 to 1804; it was acquired in 1819 for the Luxembourg museum while the artist, faithful to Napoleon, was in exile in Brussels, his authority still undisputed.

Canvas 151⅝ × 205½" (385 × 522 cm)

Antoine-Jean Gros, 1771–1835, *French*

BONAPARTE VISITING THE PLAGUE-STRICKEN AT JAFFA
(MARCH 11, 1799)

COMMISSIONED BY THE STATE, this large canvas was exhibited at the Salon of 1804, where it was acclaimed. Its intention is quite obviously that of political glorification: General Bonaparte, during the Syrian campaign in March 1799, visits the Jaffa hospital where French soldiers infected with the plague are being treated; without fearing contagion, he lingers in their presence and does not hesitate to touch them. He is shown here accompanied by Generals Berthier and Bessières, along with the surgeon Desgenettes; in the background, the French flag floats over the conquered city.

Gros, a pupil of David, achieves in this canvas, painted in only six months, a masterpiece of epic realism that largely overcomes the propagandistic purpose. The calm of the hero in the center contrasts with the anxiety of those around him. The composition by groups breaks with the frieze or pyramidal patterns employed by David's followers, as does the contrasted lighting, which joins whole areas of the canvas in half-shadow, and the warm and golden color inspired by the Venetians and Flemish. The powerful truth of such passages as the background landscape, the grandeur and pathos of the whole composition, devoid of vain melodrama as well as of artificial Oriental "local color," were admired by all, including David himself, whose *Sacre*, for its lighting effects and color, surely owes much to the *Plague-Stricken at Jaffa*. But it was on Romantic painters like Delacroix that Gros was to have a decisive influence, inspired by the violence and restlessness of his canvases, his exalted lyricism, especially in depicting the dying in the foreground shadow at the left, the density of his warm colors, the variety of his lighting effects, and the exoticism of the architecture, physical types, and costumes.

Canvas 205⅞ × 281½" (523 × 715 cm)

Théodore Géricault, 1791–1824, *French*

THE RAFT OF THE *MEDUSA*

THE RAFT OF THE MEDUSA is the first of the manifesto-paintings that appear at intervals in the history of French nineteenth-century art. The lively reactions it aroused at the time of its presentation at the Salon of 1819 bear witness to its daring novelty. Foreshadowed by the huge epic canvases of the Napoleonic campaigns by Gros (the *Plague-stricken of Jaffa,* 1804, and the *Battle of Eylau,* 1808, both at the Louvre), the work asserts the vitality of the new pictorial Romanticism.

The dynamism of its pyramidal composition, the violently contrasted lighting, its unsparing observation of a dramatized but truthful reality—all these proclaim an aggressive desire to escape from the overly judicious and impersonal equilibrium of a neoclassicism that is henceforth somewhat anemic. Michelangelo and Caravaggio are the models here, and no longer Poussin or the friezes of antiquity. The subject is a scorching contemporary event. It commemorates a tragedy that created an uproar under the Restoration, when 149 passengers of the frigate *Medusa,* shipwrecked on a raft along the coast of Africa in July 1816, were decimated (only ten or so survived) because help failed to arrive in time. The liberal opposition had made use of the scandal to accuse the government of incompetence.

Prepared for by intensive interviews with the survivors and numerous painted and drawn studies, especially from dead or dying bodies at the Beaujon hospital, the composition evokes the moment of final hope when the castaways glimpse the sail of the ship that is coming to save them.

Géricault had hoped that his painting would be bought by the state when the Salon was over, but this did not happen. Disappointed, he exhibited the canvas in London and Dublin in 1820 and 1821. Thanks, however, to Comte de Forbin, director of the royal museums, the artist's masterpiece was soon to enter the national collections. It was purchased shortly after his death in 1824.

Canvas 193⅜ × 281⅞" (491 × 716 cm)

Eugène Delacroix, 1798–1863, *French*

JULY 28: LIBERTY LEADING THE PEOPLE

AFTER THE PREMATURE DEATH of Géricault, hero of the new painting, a young artist named Eugène Delacroix brilliantly took his place. The *Massacre of Chios* (Louvre), shown at the Salon of 1824, demonstrated his prodigious technical mastery and revealed a powerful imagination, sensitive to the desperate grandeur of a contemporary tragedy. Later his interest was almost completely monopolized by subjects inspired by the East, ancient history, or certain great literary myths. *Liberty Leading the People* thus constitutes an exception in his oeuvre, since the picture illustrates an immediate public event: *"Les Trois Glorieuses,"* the three days in July 1830 that precipitated the fall of the regime of Charles X and led, after a brief hope for a republic, to the constitutional monarchy of Louis Philippe. This revolutionary flare-up had made a deep impression on people's minds. Delacroix himself, in no sense a politically committed artist, had not personally participated in the uprising, and he was overwhelmed by it. "I have undertaken a modern subject, a barricade . . . and if I haven't triumphed for my country, at least I'll paint for it," he wrote to his brother. Finished at the end of that very year, the work was exhibited at the Salon of 1831 and then bought by the state; but it seems to have contained enough subversive power for it to be withdrawn after being briefly displayed at the Luxembourg museum. The canvas was returned to Delacroix and did not reappear on permanent display at the museum until after 1861.

Rejecting the picturesque as well as the abstract, while achieving a rare combination of symbolism and the most convincing realism, Delacroix had literally brought an allegory to life. He thus created an image of universal and timeless significance that remains as disturbing and stirring as ever.

Canvas 102 × 128" (259 × 325 cm)

Eugène Delacroix, 1798–1863, *French*

THE DEATH OF SARDANAPALUS

IT WAS PROBABLY the reading of a tragedy by Byron, published at the end of 1821, that inspired Delacroix to paint *The Death of Sardanapalus*. The theme is borrowed from the ancient historian Diodorus of Sicily: Sardanapalus, a Babylonian king, besieged in his palace, prefers to immolate himself by fire with his women, his slaves, and all his riches, rather than be taken prisoner; "none of the objects that had served for his pleasure was to survive him" (Salon catalogue). But the painter himself seems to have invented the episode of the concubines massacred in the presence of the king reclining on his bed.

The *Sardanapalus*, perhaps the most ardent and lyrical example in all Romantic painting, shows the influence of Rubens on Delacroix—by its glowing color, blazing with reds and golden yellows; and by the broad movements unfurling throughout the composition like a whirlpool in which naked bodies stream. Classical space is denied; everything falls into the foreground and seems to be trying to escape the very limits of the picture. The cruel theme, which might be called sadistic, is congenial to those who cherish the Romantic sensibility: in the midst of the cataclysm and carnage that are annihilating everything he has loved, Sardanapalus, indifferent to his own destruction, gives some idea of the "spleen" of the poets of that time. But so much fever, fire, and spontaneity were long pondered, for the painter prepared for his picture with numerous drawings and studies, in pen, pencil, watercolor, and pastel, and with an overall painted sketch (Louvre). Delacroix's genius was able to preserve in his great canvas all the heat of an improvisation.

Canvas 155½ × 195¼" (395 × 496 cm)

Jean-Auguste-Dominique Ingres, 1780–1867, *French*

THE TURKISH BATH

THROUGHOUT HIS CAREER, Ingres painted bathers and odalisques—nude women, isolated in the privacy of the dressing room (*Bather of Valpinçon,* 1807, Louvre) or the luxury of the seraglio (*Odalisque with Slave,* 1839, Cambridge, Fogg Art Museum), or gathered in the stifling atmosphere of the harem (*Small Bather,* 1828, Louvre). The end of this series, and the satiation of this obsession, is *The Turkish Bath,* finished in 1862.

Long in preparation, subjected to several changes of format (it was rectangular, then square, before becoming round), the composition repeats certain elements from previous canvases and amalgamates them into a symphony of female nudes of which the history of art offers few examples so fascinating. Long considered the leader of reactionary academicism—a judgment that certain of his official attitudes and the work of several of his disciples do much to justify—Ingres here demonstrates an unalterable independence, which shows the arbitrariness of overly strict classification. By the impeccable linear flexibility of its rhythms, *The Turkish Bath* is perhaps the final homage paid by neoclassicism to the beauty of the human body; but it is just as legitimate to see it as the supreme expression of Romantic eroticism, immersed in a dream of the Orient.

Ingres sold his picture in 1865 to Khalil Bey, a Turkish diplomat residing in Paris, who also owned another masterpiece of nineteenth-century eroticism, Courbet's *Sleep* (Paris, Petit Palais). After a period of obscurity, the work reappeared in the Ingres retrospective at the Salon d'Automne of 1905. Acquired in 1911 thanks to the Société des Amis du Louvre, it has since then never ceased to arouse enthusiasm, or sometimes sneers and reprobation (Paul Claudel saw it as "a mass of women lumped together like a cake of worms"!), and to serve as a stimulus for the most diverse artists, from Picasso and the Surrealists to Rauschenberg in our own time.

Canvas 43¼ × 43¼" (110 × 110 cm)

Gustave Courbet, 1819–1877, *French*

THE PAINTER'S STUDIO

THE TUMULT AROUSED by the presentation at the Salon of 1850 of the *Burial at Ornans* (Louvre) had begun the "realist battle" and made Gustave Courbet a center of attraction. The *Studio,* the second of the artist's great manifesto-paintings, was to provoke another scandal. Indeed it was rejected by the jury at the Exposition Universelle of 1855, causing Delacroix, though he was quite remote from Courbet in both his personality and his artistic conceptions, to write: "They have turned down one of the most remarkable works of our times." Courbet then displayed the painting in a private showing of his work, in "the pavilion of realism," a temporary structure erected not far from the Exposition.

As Courbet himself wrote, the picture describes "the physical and moral history of my studio." In the center is the artist, painting a real landscape, with his naked model alongside him; to the right are his "friends," "lovers of the world of the arts," among whom can be recognized the poet Baudelaire; Champfleury, spokesman of realism; and the philosopher Proudhon. To the left is "the other world of trivial life," "the people, misery, poverty, vice, wealth, the exploited, people who live off death." The ambiguity of this program and its obscurity have given rise to many different interpretations of the subject, especially of the crowd on the left, which according to some recent critics may represent Napoleon III and his court, as well as the oppressed peoples of Europe. In any case, the multiplicity of possible interpretations demonstrates the richness of the picture, which constitutes a veritable compendium of Courbet's oeuvre (all the genres he practiced are represented, combined in a sumptuous pictorial symphony), a meditation on artistic creation itself, and an evocation, strange but profoundly suggestive, of the social and moral contradictions of his times. Courbet called his picture a "real allegory," and the paradoxical combination of words conveys perfectly the truth and poetry contained in the work.

The *Studio* entered the Louvre in 1920, thanks to a public subscription and the help of the Société des Amis du Louvre.

Canvas 142⅛ × 235½" (361 × 598 cm)

Jean-François Millet, 1814–1875, *French*

THE GLEANERS

BARBIZON, A VILLAGE situated on the edge of the forest of Fontainebleau, gave its name to a school, or rather a group, of independent painters, quite different from each other but linked by a common desire to escape from Paris and the scorn of the official world, in order to paint landscapes of the forest and plain and scenes of rural life firsthand.

Such was the case of Millet, who in 1849 joined his comrade Théodore Rousseau, who had already been living in Barbizon for two years. He was to remain there for the rest of his life. While Rousseau's subject was the forest and moors, Millet chose to describe the "epic of the fields," the dignity and suffering of the peasants.

Here, he shows three poor peasant women on the plain of Chailly. They have been excluded from the harvest, which is taking place in the background, and are only allowed to glean what the harvesters have left behind. When the painting was exhibited at the Salon of 1857, it was singled out for attack by conservative critics, who detected in it dangerous intentions of social criticism: "Behind the three gleaners are silhouetted . . . the pikes of the rioters and the scaffolds of '93," writes one of them, while another sees the gleaners as the "three Fates of pauperism."

Millet's oeuvre as a whole refutes any such interpretation. There is nothing in it to suggest either "painting with a message" or a political pamphlet, nor anything pointing the way toward the reveling in misery that the later success of naturalism was to produce. It is only a simple and grandiose vision of human labor, resting on a profound awareness of harsh contemporary reality.

Sold for 3,000 francs by Millet to a collector, *The Gleaners* was bought for 300,000 francs in 1889 by Madame Pommery, who offered it to the Louvre. The price paid for a Millet reached its maximum at that time: in 1890, Chauchard paid the fabulous sum of 800,000 francs for the famous *Angelus,* which was to enter the Louvre with the Chauchard Collection in 1909.

Canvas 32⅝ × 43¾" (83 × 111 cm)

Honoré Daumier, 1808–1879, *French*

THE WASHERWOMAN

LONG KNOWN ONLY for his numerous and admirable lithographs on satirical subjects, Daumier is also one of the great painters of the nineteenth century. The public of his time did not understand him; he lived scorned and died blind and in poverty. He was, however, admired without reserve by artists as different as Delacroix and Millet, and by such writers as Baudelaire; his friend Corot supported him in his final days.

Daumier, who lived in Paris on the Quai d'Anjou on the Île Saint-Louis, could observe the laundresses who worked at the wash house on the Seine below. It is the image of one of them, mounting the stairs with her load of laundry, and helping her little daughter up the steps, that he presents here.

The Washerwoman is one of the finest examples of Daumier's daring art, which simplifies massive and synthetic volumes, utilizes violently contrasting effects of light, and employs obvious and energetic brushwork. The squat and compact forms of the woman bending over the child, the dark outline of the silhouette standing out against a background brightly lit by the sun, the deliberately sketchy execution that blends certain portions and cross-hatches others, are all powerfully innovative aspects. This plastic strength, and still more the attitude of respect and commiseration expressed by the painter toward his characters, eloquently transforms this slender episode from everyday life into a lyrical passage of true nobility. The painting is a veritable monument raised to the labor of simple people by Daumier, who throughout his life upheld the rights of the poor. Théodore de Banville remarked in connection with this picture in 1878: "Is this not the touching and desolate image of Misery?"

Three signed versions of the *Washerwoman* exist: one, the smallest, probably figured in the Salon of 1861 (Buffalo, Albright-Knox Art Gallery); another, dated 1863, is in the Metropolitan Museum. The one in the Louvre, the most simplified and monumental, was purchased at the P. Bureau auction in 1927; it dates from between 1861 and 1863.

Panel 19¼ × 12¾" (49 × 32.5 cm)

Jean-Baptiste-Camille Corot, 1796–1875, *French*

INTERIOR OF SENS CATHEDRAL

COROT WAS SEVENTY-EIGHT when he painted this canvas, probably the last one he painted on the spot, in three sessions in September 1874. He was to die a few months later.

Still capable of renewing his inspiration—he had just painted the admirable *Lady in Blue* (Louvre)—he shows the undiminished freshness of his "synthesizing and abbreviating gaze," as Baudelaire called it, and a sort of pictorial gaiety. Here he once again forgets the misty foliage and poetic shade trees, perhaps repeated too often, that had assured his fame, and paints for himself something quite new, of which there is scarcely but one other example in his immense oeuvre (the *Cathedral of Mantes*), a church interior vibrant with light. Despite the similarity in composition, nothing here recalls the skillful constructions of the seventeenth-century Dutch, nor the picturesque cathedrals of the Romantics. Painted with the tip of the brush, with a verve and a lightness of touch that justifies the statement by his friend the painter Daubigny, "You've put in nothing, but everything is there," the work conveys a pure visual impression. Enlivening the diaphanous yellow of the background, the indispensable red spot of the beadle's vestment (Father Marquet, who, according to an often cited anecdote, is supposed to have insisted on appearing in the picture) balances the pure colors of the windows.

The Louvre owns more than 130 works by Corot, for the most part from large collections of nineteenth-century paintings given to it at the beginning of this century, in particular the Thomy Thiéry (1902), Moreau-Nélaton (1906), and Chauchard (1909) collections. *Sens Cathedral* was a gift from Jacques Zoubaloff in 1919.

Canvas 24 × 15¾" (61 × 40 cm)

EDITOR'S NOTE

AS MICHEL LACLOTTE HAS NOTED in his introduction, the Louvre has profited from over four hundred years of collecting by the kings and nobility of royal France, and later by private citizens who donated their pictures to the Museum.

The Louvre's collection spans centuries and crosses borders: from the Early and High Renaissance in Europe to the Barbizon school in the mid-nineteenth century. In its galleries are contained some of the most important examples of painting from continental Europe, Britain, and America.

To present a more complete overview of the Louvre's vast collection, we have added twenty-seven paintings covering the full chronological and geographical span of the Louvre's holdings. Some are by artists whose work has already been commented on; others are by artists whose work provides particularly fine examples of periods and styles discussed by the authors.

MARTINI – Christ on the Road to Calvary
(1280–1344) Panel 9½ × 6¼"

FRA FILIPPO LIPPI – Madonna with Angels
(1406–1469) Panel 85½ × 96"

TURA – Pietà
(1430–1495) Panel 52 × 105⅛"

MANTEGNA – Our Lady of Victories
(1430–1506) Canvas 110¼ × 69½″

MEMLING – Triptych (Resurrection)
(1430–1494) Panel 24 × 32″

TERBORCH – Young Woman with Soldier
(1617–1681) Canvas 26⅜ × 21⅝″

PERUGINO – Apollo and Marsyas
(1448–1523) Panel 15⅜ × 11⅜″

MORO – Cardinal Granvelle's Dwarf
(1517–1576) Panel 50 × 36⅝″

METSU – The Vegetable Market
(1629–1667) Canvas 37⅜ × 32⅞″

RENI – Rape of Deiarira
(1576–1642) Canvas 94 × 76″

VAN DYCK – Madonna with Donors
(1599–1641) Canvas 98½ × 75″

HOLBEIN – Portrait of Nicolas Kratzer
(1497–1543) Panel 32½ × 26½″

PIAZZETTA – The Assumption of the Virgin
(1683–1754) Canvas 203½ × 98½″

REMBRANDT – The Pilgrims at Emmaus
(1606–1669) Panel 26⅜ × 25⅜″

FRIEDRICH – Tree with Ravens
(1774–1840) Canvas 23¼ × 29½″

RIBERA – The Club-Footed Boy
(1591–1652) Canvas 64½ × 36¼"

BELLECHOSE– Last Communion of St. Denis
(Active 1415–1444) Panel 63⅜ × 82⅝

ROBERT– Louvre in Ruins: Imaginary View
(1733–1808) Canvas 40 × 35"

MIRANDA– Mass for the Trinitaires
(1614–1685) Canvas 196⅞ × 128¾"

CLOUET – Portrait of Francis I
(1485–1572) Panel 37¾ × 29"

WATTEAU– Gilles
(1684–1721) Canvas 72½ × 58¾"

LAWRENCE– Sir S.J. Angerstein and Wife
(1769–1830) Canvas 100 × 62¼"

RIGAUD– Portrait of Louis XIV
(1659–1743) Canvas 110 × 94¾"

INGRES– Portrait of Monsieur Bertin
(1780–1867) Canvas 45⅝ × 37⅜"

BONINGTON– Versailles: Water Parterre
(1802–1828) Canvas 16½ × 20½"

VALENTIN– Concert au bas-relief antique
(1594–1632) Canvas 84¼ × 68⅛"

J.-L. DAVID– Consecration of Napoleon I
(1748–1825) Canvas 240 × 366½"